TROOPER TALES

STORIES OF THE ILLINOIS STATE POLICE

By

John R. Gossett, Ph.D.

© 2019 John R. Gossett   All rights reserved.
ISBN: 9781795448925

INTRODUCTION

If you are reading this small book, "Thank you." My name is John Gossett and I spent a little over 25 years as a State policeman in Illinois. My career started as an Illinois Secretary of State Police officer, followed by the Illinois Commerce Commission Police officer, and then finished as a State Trooper. All three jobs required I make traffic stops up and down the state highways of Illinois. I worked in all the lower 32 counties regularly and many of the ones further north including Cook County for a short period. The result of my work is this short volume named "Trooper Tales."

Trooper tales is so named because it is a catchy title but more importantly because I cannot remember all the details exactly. I don't think anyone could look back to 1987 (the year I started as a policeman) from 2018 and get all the details perfect.

This book is my very best recollection of a number of funny, sad, and interesting, set of events that occurred in my life. So with that said I hope you enjoy a series of short stories called "Trooper Tales."

CHAPTER 1
ACADEMY BOXING

Academies teach newly hired police officers many needed skills. For example, the police need to know both traffic law and criminal law. Police also need to know case law. Case law is found in court decisions. You readers know about the Miranda warning. The Miranda warning is found in the case of Miranda versus Arizona. All of what I have listed so far is academic stuff. The academies go well beyond academics and get into the skills of everyday policing such as high speed pursuit driving, handcuffing, shooting, and self-defense.

Self-defense is taught by special instructors at the Illinois State police academies. These trainers are themselves taught by people with very special skills and receive certificates to allow them to teach the newly hired officers. We spent weeks on self- defense. At the end of the training, the cadets are paired off to fight with other cadets in their respective weight classes. I am writing of two of these fights.

One of my fellow cadets, we will call William, was formerly a professional boxer. In his fight with his opponent (a former professional football player), William won rather convincingly. One of our instructors was a beautiful woman in her late 20's. The instructor had us hold a striking bag up and she jumped into the air and did a triple spin and struck the bag with a great deal of force. The lady wanted to fight William.

While William was not a chauvinist, he did not want to fight the instructor. He pleaded with the staff to consider that he outweighed the instructor by 60 plus pounds. He argued while this young lady knew Kung Fu, he was a former pro boxer. He could see that the staff was not listening and said really he did not wish to hit a woman. The last argument about hitting a woman brought scorn from the staff that he was not up with the times.

William was sent to the ring to face the female instructor. The woman jumped into the air and did her roundabout but missed. William then threw a right punch. William hit the instructor so hard she flew out of the ring area. The lady had two black eyes and was taken from the fight area and given first aid. When we graduated two weeks or so later the instructor was still sporting two black eyes.

The second story happened this same day and I was one of the two fighters. I was paired with a new police officer from the Chicago area. My opponent was a weight lifter and was more muscular than I was. I had a slight reach advantage from being taller than my opponent.

When the fight started, I quickly realized I had a major disadvantage in that I'm very near sighted and could not wear my glasses. I pressed my opponent and he was backing away, but as I pressed him I was made to pay dearly as he kept hitting me in the face. My face was bruising up badly but I pressed on. Right before the end of round one (we fought three rounds of three minutes apiece), I landed a hard right. My opponent collapsed. I had knocked him unconscious.

I don't know if my opponent had a glass jaw or I really punch that hard, but this guy was out. The staff brought smelling salts to my opponent to wake him from his unconscious state. My opponent was not permanently injured. My opponent certainly looked better that the lady instructor William had hit.

CHAPTER 2
THE RED ROCK

Marching is a skill I personally find little use for. The military and the Illinois State Police must disagree as marching is a high priority item to both. The Illinois State Police spend weeks teaching the correct method of marching. Every morning at the academy, the cadets are lined up in formation and the marching drills commence. I did two academies and this is a story regarding the red rock which occurred during my first academy.

People who believe marching is a needed skill will tell you marching is the easiest way to get a large number of people to the same destination. After the academy, I never marched again so I doubt this skill is really a requirement for a good policeman. Never the less, at the academy, marching is used, and I was not very good at it as an incoming cadet. When everyone else was on their left foot, I was on my right. I was so bad that my academy class had three platoons of twelve men and one platoon of just me. I was put in my own platoon because in any other platoon of more people I just screwed it up. I was a good runner. Every morning in addition to marching we would run several miles. One of my overseers came up to me as I was running one day and said it was a good thing I could run well because I sure could not march.

The overseers got so mad at me that one day one of them appeared with a baseball sized red rock. I was told this was to be with me at all times in my left hand. I was to eat with it, sleep with it, run with it, and shower with it. If I were to ever be caught without the red rock in my left hand, I was told I would be disciplined. The red rock was to teach me my left side from my right side.

For six weeks I lived with my red rock. I literally slept with it, showered with it, and kept it in my left hand. After six weeks a transformation took place in my marching skills. I cannot explain why but I picked up the skill. (I doubt it had anything to do with the rock but then again who knows).

I was called into the overseer's office. I was told to hand in my red rock. I was congratulated for my new marching skills. I noticed the overseer looking closely at the rock. He spun the rock around and continued to look closely at it. Finally the overseer looked at me and said I had lost the original rock and replaced it with another similar rock. He was visibly upset as he saw me as a cheater.

I explained this was the original rock. I asked why he would accuse me of losing the original and replacing it.

The overseer said he had hidden his initials on the rock and they were not on the rock I had just turned in.

I said: " look, I have showered for six weeks with this red rock, I suppose your initials were washed off. If the initials did not wash off it is possible I wore them off from the carrying it in my hand for six weeks. I don't know for sure why your initials are not visible but I do know I did not change out your rock."

With a sheepish look, the overseer accepted my explanation. Even he knew putting initials on a rock being carried for six weeks and then expecting to find them was a bad idea.

CHAPTER 3
THE DEAD SPIDER

Academies are the boot camps for Police. While a great deal of necessary preparation takes place for the individual officer, there is an attempt by most academies to instill unquestioned obedience to orders from superiors. The means for creating unquestioned obedience is usually in the form of punishment for even the smallest offenses. If a cadet or recruit has an improperly shined shoe, that violation could mean 50 pushups. Not standing in formation properly could lead to being put in front leaning rest (here you are in the top of a pushup) for five minutes. If a cadet doesn't mess up much, the staff will invent something so as to instill blind obedience to orders. If the staff doesn't like you the result will be many punishments.

One punishment we all hated was being given a memo to write. The memo would have to be a certain length, and have no errors. If an error is found in the memo, the staff circles it with a big red pen and ships it back to the cadet for a rewrite. For example, on day one you get a memo to write for being late for class. On day two it comes back to you with a mistake and has to be rewritten. On day two your shoe had a smudge on it so you get assigned a memo. Now on day two you are writing in effect two memos (the original and the rewrite). These rewrites back up and now each day you have more to write and rewrite. You feel very angry but cannot complain. The staff are creating artificial stress (as they call it) to see if you will keep obeying orders.

On the day in question one of my fellow cadets got in trouble. The fellow tended to be somewhat foolish acting and the staff had picked up on it. They were looking for reasons to create him grief. A spider had died on his bunk bed blanket. The fellow was called in by staff to see the dead spider. The staff then demanded the cadet produce a 100 word memo on what had caused the death of the spider on his blanket.

The poor cadet came to me almost in tears. He had a limited ability to do creative writing and had no idea of how to come up with 100 words on how the spider had died. He knew if he did not produce the memo many pushups awaited him.

I told the guy to calm down as I would assist him. I said to define a spider. I said to differentiate a spider from an insect (spiders have eight legs while insects have six). Then I gave him an outline. Start by saying the spider might have died of old age. Perhaps the spider had a heart attack from advanced age. Then I suggested the spider might have died from the chemicals the exterminator had been spraying in the building for bugs. Finally I suggested he point out the academy was incredibly cold and perhaps the poor spider had died due to the cold (this was a little dig at the staff making us uncomfortable on purpose.)

The lad began to write. Using my outline he easily got past the required 100 word mark. We double checked the memo for errors and he shipped it in.

The next day my cadet buddy was again almost in tears. I asked the problem and he pulled out the memo I had assisted him with. Although the staff could find no errors in spelling, punctuation, or word length, they had written rewrite on the original memo. The reason for the rewrite was in bright red ink. My friend had not cited Webster's dictionary as a source for his definition of a spider.

See I told you they were out to get my friend.

CHAPTER 4
TRAINING FOR HIGH-SPEED CAR PURSUITS

High speed car pursuits are terrifying. Any officer who says otherwise is missing something in the head. The Illinois State Police Academy attempts to provide the necessary training to not only survive a pursuit but to win one. (Winning means to stay with the fleeing vehicle until the perpetrator stops or crashes and can be arrested)

The Illinois State Police have a small racetrack at their Pawnee Illinois pistol range. It is a circular track with multiple turns on it. On each curve is a rectangular box that has been painted on the asphalt. The boxes are used to rate the drivers as they race around the track. The drivers are required to make laps around the track in a designated amount of time. In addition to beating the clock, the driver must put two wheels across each painted box that he comes to (remember there is one box per curve). Failure to hit the required box results in a loss of points. A 70% score is required along with a certain speed (time).

Professional race car drivers know techniques that can increase police speed and handling on the curves. For instance, all braking is done prior to the curve. The braking plus a slight turn of the wheel makes the cars weight shift ever so slightly allowing for a higher speed on a given curve. If properly practiced it gives law enforcement a leg up on the bad guys we are pursuing.

Other training includes reaction skills. One drill is to send a car down a straight-a-way at about 65 miles per hour. At the end of the track there are three lanes. Each lane is controlled by a traffic light.

As the trainee speeds down the straight-a-way the light to the far left may be green , while the middle lane is red, and the right lane is also red. In the just listed case, the driver would turn his steering wheel a full half turn left, throw the car into a skid, and then shoot through the left lane. Other situations might be that the right lane would be green and the other two lanes red requiring the driver to go right. The simplest situation is when the center lane is green and other lanes are red here the driver simply goes through the center.

On the day we were training on the reaction skills test the range itself was in use. Our straight-a-way had squad cars parked on it from officers that were practicing entry skills in a pretend house just off the straight-a-way. Thus vision was limited as we raced down toward our reaction lanes. One of my Cadet friends, John Hartsick had just gone down the track. The reaction lighting had caused him take the far right lane. He was then forced to go across all the lanes to get to the far left to proceed back up the straight-a-way. In the mean time I could not see John but figured he must be out of the way and I went up to 65 mph as I was racing to the reaction lights. My mind was on the lights and not John. The lights sent me to the far left lane. Unfortunately John was still on the track in front of me as I shot down my lane. I hit John at a very high speed totaling both cars.

Safety had not been a big item on the day I crashed my car with John's car. None of the cars parked on the straight-a-way should have been allowed to park there. Those parked cars affected the visibility of those practicing reaction skills. John should not have been forced to cross all lanes of traffic to return back to the starting point of the maneuver. We had been given a radio code called code red. When any trainee or trainer saw an issue this code was to be called and all traffic was to stop immediately. No code red was given. Needless to say the trainers were upset. They had just lost two squad cars worth thousands of dollars

The following day Colonel Jableski came out to the training grounds. The Colonel walked all over the academy training grounds looking for the two wrecked cars. He said he wanted to see the two vehicles involved in the fender bender (he had been intentionally misled by his underling officers). When the Colonel located the cars, I could hear him yelling at the staff that this was no fender bender. He declared the cars totaled (which they were) and wanted to know who was keeping him misinformed. Needless to say this added to the staff's anger at me for being the driver that was involved in the training crash.

When the day came for me to pass the speed driving test, I flashed through the track in record time. When my score came in on putting two wheels across each box, I was promptly failed. The instructor's claimed I had missed too many boxes.

Quite frankly I did not believe the scorers. I figured they were still sore over Colonel Jableski jumping their case over the lies they had told concerning the two totaled squad cars. I ended up doing 50 pushups with my feet elevated on the bumper of a squad car. These guys had no sense of humor. The staff did finally pass me on the road test. My score was the lowest one they could give me and still let me pass. I got a 70%. As I set here writing this many years later I still chuckle at the staff's anger. All their efforts to get even were for naught as I retired a Trooper just like they did.

CHAPTER 5
A BLEEDING NAKED MAN

Mental illness is a tragic thing. I have met people who struggle with this daily. While some drugs can make a difference, it seems to me that once a person in inflicted with mental illness it lasts a lifetime. Not only does the inflicted person suffer but so does the family of that person. This is a story of my dealing with a man with mental illness.

I was on IL Rt 149 in West Frankfort, Illinois. It was near midnight on a cool fall evening and I had stopped a driver of a car at the railroad track in the center of this small community. The driver had a taillight out and I had the driver come to my squad car and sit with me as I wrote his warning citation. After 11 P.M. I would always have violators sit with me in my squad car as it increased my opportunity to spot a drunk driver.

Next to the railroad track is a very old apartment building that served as a hotel during the early part of the 20th century. This apartment building housed the very poorest of West Frankfort's citizens due to its poor condition and low rent. As I wrote the warning citation, some interested citizens from the apartment building would look on out of curiosity and boredom.

About the time I released my driver with his warning citation he said, "did you see that!"

I replied did I see what?

The driver said, "a bleeding naked man... did you see him just run behind that apartment building?"

Not only did I not see the bleeding naked man, I doubted the story. I was thinking this driver is trying to get away from me. So instead of responding to the bleeding guy I double checked my driver for sobriety. My driver was sober so I proceeded to see if I could find the bleeding guy.

I notified radio I needed backup and went to the rear of the apartment building. Behind the apartment, to the west, is an alley and sure enough there was a naked guy covered in blood. I went to him and he had cut both wrists deeply with a knife. Luckily, this man, like most people who attempt suicide with a knife, did not know what he was doing. Amateurs cut their wrist horizontally to the arm and the blood is fairly quickly stopped as the body can coagulate it. If the wrist would have been cut vertically with the arm, I am sure this guy would have died.

I grabbed my portable radio and asked for an ambulance. The ambulance arrived in seconds as we were only two blocks from the firehouse where it was kept. My backup officer must have been coming from further away as he arrived much later.

The man was mumbling about sexual stuff but was not uncooperative. I got him to sit on a gurney brought by the ambulance personnel. I could see my backup officer had arrived so I motioned for him to come to assist me but he stayed back and did not come to assist me.

We got the bleeding man to lay on the gurney and put nylon belts across his body. These belts keep patients from falling off the gurney. In this case I wanted to get the belts across this man as soon as possible. I realized he was mentally disturbed and know such people are often have unbelievable strength.

We no more than got the straps on and the bleeding guy tried to break free. Those straps are about 4 inches across and can supposedly hold 4,000 pounds of push. I swear I thought this guy was going to break the straps. He pushed upward with all the strength he could muster and the straps stretched but did not break. The man was taken to our local hospital. I got with his family and it was a heartbreaking experience. This family had dealt with this kind of behavior for years and it appeared it would continue.

I then got with my backup officer. I wanted to know why he did not come to me when I waved him to come to me.

The backup guy said he thought my bleeding man was mentally disturbed.

I replied that was correct but what did that have to do with his not coming to assist me.

The backup officer said "you know those mentally disturbed people are really strong and can hurt you."

I said, "Yes I know that and that is why I needed you." Go figure!

CHAPTER 6
A CHASE THROUGH THE WOODS AFTER A NURSE

Police officers and nurses always seem to get along well. Oftentimes car wrecks or other emergencies bring the two professions together. The result of the meeting is often romance. I have known several male police officers who married nurses. Nurses therefore are a noble profession in my eyes. The story of this nurse is then the exception to the rule in terms of nursing morals.

I was called to a wreck on I57 in Williamson County. The wreck occurred where the Lake of Egypt almost touches the interstate. Although the lake is hidden by trees, it comes to within a football field of the highway for a distance of about a mile.

When I arrived at the accident scene, I saw a car had smashed into the rear of a truck tractor trailer unit. I got out of the car and the truck driver was telling me the driver of the car was a male dressed in green scrubs and had grabbed a trash bag from his car and ran into the woods.

I called for backup and jumped the fence that runs beside the highway and went running the direction the truck driver said the man in scrubs had went. I knew the suspect could not go very far from the highway due to the location of the lake. I was young and fit and was a good runner, so I ran the mile in the woods that parallels the lake but did not find my suspect.

I stopped. I thought the average man could not have covered this mile as fast as I had, so I returned toward the direction of the traffic accident. I found a hollow (a dip in the topography) and my suspect was sitting on a log trying to get his breath. I drew my gun and told the suspect not to do anything rash or he would be shot. I got the suspect handcuffed.

I marched the suspect from the wood onto the highway. A group of five troopers had assembled in response for my request for backup. I took the handcuffs off my suspect and took him through a series of field sobriety test. The suspect was on drugs and had alcohol in his system.

I arrested my suspect for DUI on drugs and alcohol. He was a nurse at a nearby hospital and was en route to work. The nurse refused to admit he took a bag into the woods. I suspected it contained drugs but could not locate it.

My disappointment with this case was that it involved a nurse: especially a nurse going to work who was inebriated. I am actually thankful for the crash in which no one was injured. This crash may have well prevented a far more serious injury to an unsuspecting hospital patient.

CHAPTER 7
A DRUNK WOMAN WITH A CRAZY LAWYER

Lawyers are a different type of people. They are without exception intelligent. Sometimes the lawyers use their intelligence in a way that benefits society. They often craft good laws or use the courtroom to find justice for the injured. As I see it, too often lawyers prey upon the down and out and hurting or attempt to cause a miscarriage of justice. Many lawyers use divorce courts not to find a solution to the problem in the marriage but to continue the courtroom saga till both their client and the ex-spouse are broke. In continuing the courtroom saga, these layers line their pockets with cash from the marriage problems of others. Similarly many defense attorneys do not expect to win their case but rather to prolong it so as to get the largest payoff from their client. The story I am about to tell appeared to me to be a lawyers search not for justice but for cash.

On the night in question I was traveling into Marion, Illinois on Il Rt 37 from the south side of the city. I got behind a yellow Buick that was weaving badly. I followed the Buick as it turned west onto a side street. I activated my overheads and got the Buick to stop.

The lady driving was intoxicated. I got her from the car and she had to lean upon me for support to prevent falling over. The lady wanted me to call her daughter and have her come a few blocks and drive the car. I refused to consider this as she was under arrest for DUI.

I took the lady to the sheriff's office. Once here she began to enjoy herself. She began to sing loudly and tried to get the janitor to join her in song. She grabbed the poor guy and began to force him to move along with her as she danced. I noted her festive actions in my report.

In spite of all her crazy actions the lady surprised me and blew into the breathalyzer machine. The machine showed this lady was three times over the limit for blood alcohol in Illinois. I suppose her intoxication made her happy in spite of her being under arrest.

The lady got one of the more active DUI lawyers from Marion to take her case. This was a case where the lawyer should have known there was no chance to win but he proceeded anyway. I received a summon to court and braced myself as this attorney was always coming up with a different angle to win cases.

I arrived at court and we went through all the normal hoopla. The attorney tried in pretrial motions to get my field sobriety test thrown out. When that did not work, we finally ended up in trial.

Under questioning from the states attorney, I was using the woman's singing and dancing as a sign she was intoxicated. My argument was that in addition breathalyzers report, the very fact a person would sing and dance while at jail under arrest was a sure sign of her being drunk.

Mr. Defense Attorney had a whole different take on the lady's singing and dancing. He asked me if I knew the woman's occupation. I replied she was a bar maid. He asked me what bar maids do. I replied they serve drinks to those in a bar. Yes the defense attorney replied that is true but you are missing the bigger picture. Bar maids are in the entertainment industry so it only makes since that she would sing and dance even at the jail. Then after making his observation of bar maids being in the entertainment industry he put the situation to me in the form of a question. "Officer Gossett, now that you know that bar maids are entertainers, doesn't it make sense to you that this lady would sing even while under arrest?

I replied that was the stupidest argument I had ever heard.

I could almost feel the judge glaring at me. I think when these attorneys make really stupid arguments we as police are not allowed to point out how stupid they are. Well if that was the case I just violated the unwritten agreement. No, bar maids aren't professional singers, they deliver drinks. Further if this particular bar maid had any sobriety in her she would not have sang and danced while under arrest for DUI.

Well I won this case. I am sure the breathalyzer reading won it more than my argument on the bar maids singing.

A few years later I ran into the gung ho defense attorney. I had heard he had quit being an attorney. I asked if he had quit being an attorney and he said he had. The lawyer said too many of his clients had stiffed him on his fee for representing them. I reminded him of the bar maid trial. Yes he said she had stiffed him of his fee too. I felt like saying I hope she entertained you with her act of being a paying client... but I didn't!

CHAPTER 8
A GOTH IN THE CEMETERY

In case you have never met a goth, let me describe them to you. They are into heavy metal dark music. They dye their hair jet black and wear black clothing. The young man in this story wore white face makeup with black eyeliner and black eye shadow. His dress (yes that's correct) was black lace and he had fingerless black gloves on. He wore black "fairy" looking boots.

On the night I met the goth, I was driving on Il RT 37 at Il Rt 13 in Williamson County. There is a large cemetery at this location and it has an old church structure on the cemetery grounds. It was 1 A.M. and I was tired. I looked at the old church, which is lit by streetlights, and saw a pickup truck and a smaller car facing each other in the church parking area. The pickup took off and rammed he car. The car went backwards as if it were now in reverse. The pickup shot forward again and hit the rear moving car.

I turned on overhead lights and went to investigate. I called in what I had observed and went to the pickup driver. The pickup driver was a farm kid. He said he was angry at his friend in the car for chasing him all over Marion tonight. He said he had hid out in the cemetery just to be alone and the car's driver had followed him into the cemetery. He said his friend was getting too weird to be around anymore.

I walked over to the car. I intended to speak to the car's driver about chasing the farm boy all over town. I shined my light inside the car and know I jumped three feet in the air. It was 1 A.M., I was in a cemetery, I had just observed an out of the ordinary car crash, and now I was looking at what appeared to be a corpse driving this car.

Once I got control of myself, I spoke with the young man. He said he was a "goth" and admitted a fascination with dark things like death. He said the farm boy was his last friend and he had just wanted to talk with him and meant no harm by chasing him.

The car had serious damage and I had to do a cash report. As I was working on the report, a Marion officer arrived. He asked if he could do anything for me. Since I knew the officer I decided I had to have a little fun. I told him to go check on the driver of the car but to be careful as I considered him dangerous (not true but I needed a ruse to get him over by the car).

The Marion officer went to the car and shined his flashlight in. I saw the officer jump about three feet in the air like I had earlier. I called out to my fellow officer, "you're a little jumpy tonight, huh!"

I ended up finishing the crash report and cited the farm boy for improper lane usage. This was a minor charge. I could have used reckless driving or reckless conduct but decided to give him a break. I cited the goth for not having a valid license. I did the crash report describing this as a deliberate act by both boys. I bet their respective insurance companies did a double take on this accident.

CHAPTER 9
A RICH MAN AND HIS WATCHES

Solomon was the wisest person who ever lived. Solomon says in Proverbs 18:23, "The poor man pleads for mercy but the rich man answers harshly." I have seen the above acted out many times in my life as a policeman. I would arrest a poor man and he would just plead again and again for mercy. The poor man would say, "Can't you just let me go this time, I will never do this again." The rich man would threaten me with his political connections and his power. I would often hear such statements as "do you know who I am." The rich man would be angry, even indignant, that I dare arrest him. This is a story on a rich man who got so angry he actually died over my lack of perceived care of his watches.

I was on patrol on I64 near Nashville, Illinois on a Friday night in 1995. Traffic was heavy even at this late hour (11 P.M.) due to people traveling home from a St. Louis Cardinal Baseball game that recently concluded. I observed a red Cadillac going Eastbound that was going across the two Eastbound lanes. Since this was in 1995 before the advent of cell phones, a driver such as the one in the red Cadillac that was having trouble staying in its lane indicated a sleepy driver or a drunk driver.

I switched on my overhead lights and the Cadillac finally got to the emergency stop lane. I went forward and spoke to the driver. I could smell the heavy odor of alcoholic beverages coming from the driver's breath. Rather than talk about his driving, the driver wanted me to know he was a professional golfer. He also wanted me to know he was good friends with President "Bill Clinton." The driver was from Little Rock Arkansas and claimed he taught President Bill Clinton how to properly play golf.

Every time I spoke to my suspect he would mention President Bill Clinton. My suspect was correct that Mr. Clinton was currently President but I doubted a strong friendship. I explained to my suspect that Mr. Clinton might be President but that would have no bearing on his case here.

I took the suspect through the field sobriety tests and he was very intoxicated. I put him in handcuffs and went through his car in order to put all his valuables on an inventory sheet. I took note of what appeared to be very expensive golf clubs in the trunk. Also in the trunk were 10 or so watches. I always made sure to properly inventory any car whose driver I was taking to jail. That inventory sheet protected me and the tow truck driver from claims of theft.

The tow truck came and took away the Cadillac. I then drove toward the county jail in Nashville. As we neared the county jail the suspect asked me where I had put his watches. I explained the watches went with his car to the tow yard. I explained I had put his watches on the inventory sheet so the they would be accounted for.

My suspect came unglued. He said that these watches were Rolexes and were worth a half million dollars. He said I was a piece of crap and I would not ever be worth what these watches were worth. The suspect was ranting that I should have brought the watches with us.

By now we had arrived at the jail. I opened the car door and took the suspect out.

The suspect now yells, "My heart, my pills." He falls to the ground with me holding on enough to break the fall. I reach down and check his carotid artery in his neck and this guy is dead. No sign of a heartbeat.

I think of doing CPR but decide to get the Emergency Medical Technicians (EMT's) from the basement of the same jail I'm at. I run to the basement and yell "man down and we need an Automated External Defibrillator (AED)."

Now the EMT's come hastily to the scene. They are half dressed because they hang out in the basement of the jail and certainly were not expecting this situation. In 1995 the AED's were antiquated compared to today. The paddles they used back then were similar to air hockey paddles kids play at arcades now. These paddles were scary things. I imagined I could hear the electricity humming in them back then. The EMT's jerk the suspect's shirt apart and apply the paddles. The suspect's body arches about 6" on each application of the paddles. On the third hit of the paddles my suspect begins to breathe.

As I'm watching this scene unfold a jailer joins me. We both watch the suspect's body contort from the application of the shock paddles. We watch this contortion take place three times. The voltage in those paddles must be pretty high to restart a heart. Never the less, the jailer looks at me and remarks, "I think he is faking, don't you."

Incredulously I respond," No I think he has really had a heart attack."

The breathing suspect is put on a gurney for transport to a hospital. I meet the EMT's at the hospital in Nashville. I fill out my paperwork but my Master Sergeant overrules my desire to take a blood sample. The Master Sergeant is afraid the guy will die again and doesn't want us taking blood from a dying man.

Well this guy did not die. The following morning he drove home to Arkansas. I had no blood to convict him with and he probably got a reckless driving charge instead of the DUI he deserved.

Hey, maybe that jailer was right. Maybe he was faking.

CHAPTER 10
A SECOND CHANCE

    Everybody wants a second chance in life. You screw something up and you just hope to get a chance to get it right later. This feeling is universal. Police mess up too. I messed up in this story but got a chance to make it right.

    I was passing the Marion, Illinois exit on Interstate 57 going Northbound. I looked down on IL. Rt. 13 (a road that intersects I57) and could see a green pickup coming up the ramp to come onto I57. The truck was going to merge with me. I scooted over to the passing lane to leave the slower driving lane to the green pickup as it merged into I57. The truck went across the driving lane and into the passing lane. This sudden crossing of two lanes was illegal as the law requires giving adequate room to other traffic when changing lanes. I certainly wasn't given adequate room as I had to veer into the median to avoid a car crash.

    I activated my warning lights and followed the truck for a mile. The truck was all over the highway as I followed it for the mile. Finally the driver pulled to the roadways edge.

    I went forward to the violator's truck. I was thinking I was probably dealing with a drunk. Bingo! Driver's very intoxicated. The driver fails the field sobriety tests and is arrested. The truck is towed and off we go to the jail.

    At the jail, I read the violator his "warning to motorist." The warning to motorist is a legal document that tells the violator the penalties for giving breath in a breathalyzer machine and being over . 08 in blood alcohol content. The penalty here is a one year driver's license suspension. The warning to motorist also tells the penalty for refusing to blow in the breath machine. The penalty for refusing to blow is a six months driver's license suspension. Finally the warning to motorist says there is no penalty if a person's blood alcohol content comes in under .08 percent.

The wording in the warning to motorist is very hard to understand. The warning to motorist was written by lawyers and is impossible for most sober people to understand, much less a person who has consumed alcohol.

When this drunk asked what the warning to motorist meant I attempted to explain it as I did above. If your over .08 don't take the test for you will be suspended a year. Take the test if you are under .08 because you will not be suspended. Refuse the test and you get a six month suspension automatically and only do this if you think you are over the limit.

My drunk wanted to call his lawyer. I said fine and handed him the phone. He called his lawyer and got no answer. I handed him the phone book and he tried calling several other lawyers without reaching any. Finally I started the machine. I said this is your call......either breath in it or don't breath in it. If you don't breathe in the machine, I'm calling it a refusal. The arrestee refused to breath in it and I wrote on the warning to motorist that he had refused to take the breath test. The arrestee was now set to get a six month suspension.

The arrestee got a very good local attorney. I was summoned to a probable cause Secretary of State hearing before a judge. At this hearing, the judge would see if I had followed the law correctly in making this stop and handing out the six month suspension. The judge found I had probable cause to make the stop due to the arrestee's truck being in my lane. The judge ruled that when I allowed the arrestee to call his attorney I had erred. If I allowed a single call to an attorney, I would have to allow as many calls to as many attorneys as this arrestee wished to make. The judge said while I had gone beyond the norm in helping this drunk, I had accidentally given him an out. The judge gently reprimanded me for being so nice. The judge said in the future only read the warning to motorist to the violator and do not interpret it. Finally the judges said do not allow the arrestee to call his/her attorney prior to the decision to give a breath sample. The judge said he would hand down a final ruling in a few days.

I felt like I had been hit with a hammer. I had did my very best to be fair and instead jeopardized my arrest. I was looking for a second chance.

The following day I had a different case at the same county courthouse. I arrived and took a seat. To my surprise my arrestee whom I had been in court with the previous day was also there. The arrestee's lawyer was arguing for this man to be allowed to drive today prior to the judge's written decision and a Secretary of State reinstatement. The judge told the attorney he would have to await the written ruling that was due in a few days.

I could not believe my good luck. I had just heard the judge in effect say this guy is still suspended till you get my decision in writing and that decision is not complete yet.

I went to the basement of the courthouse. I located that same old green truck my defendant had driven the night I had arrested him for DUI. I called the court security guard over. I explained my arrest of a man I had just observed in court. I explained that man was still suspended because I just heard it come from the judge's mouth. I explained I needed a witness if my DUI arrestee attempted to drive that old green truck home from the courthouse.

Sure enough my arrestee came out of the courthouse. He was looking this way and that to see if I was around. Little did he know I was watching him from the courthouse basement with a witness.

The arrestee got in his truck and drove to the roadways edge from the courthouse parking lot. I slipped out of the courthouse basement and when he hit the street driving, I am in a full run. I am running beside his truck telling him to pull over. The man looks at me and speeds up. My car is parked just ahead so I jump in it and give chase. The arrestee has decided to pull in a business and is trying to walk away as if he hasn't driven his truck. I jump out of my squad car and handcuff him. I tow his truck again. I take him to jail for driving while suspended. He lacks bond and is jailed.

I heard through the grapevine the arrestee's attorney was furious at me. The deputy who saw the attorney's reaction said he kept saying this arrest is "chicken shit".

You really can't blame the attorney for being upset. After all, the attorney's hard work at getting the suspension removed was worthless. The arrestee was now revoked instead of suspended. A revocation is far worse than a suspension. A revocation means if this man is caught driving again the penalty is an automatic eight days in jail; where driving with a suspension carries no automatic jail time. A revocation is for a minimum of one year where this man's suspension was for six months.

In addition to all the above difficulties my arrestee faced, I got to tow his truck a second time and jail him again. Both of these acts on my part cost him many more dollars. Dollars for the second bond and dollars to pay the second tow bill. Oh yes, I got a second chance.

CHAPTER 12
A TRUCK IN THE POND

In Southern Illinois good jobs are scarce. There is little manufacturing here and the population is so thin even service sector jobs are tough to come by. One job that stands out in Southern Illinois is truck driving. The area has some minerals, which allows for some local hauling, and the several interstate highways pass through the area, allowing local people to be employed by over the road trucking companies. To be a truck driver and lose your job, means serious economic problems for the former driver and his/her family.

I received a radio alert of a truck in a pond East of Pinckneyville, Illinois on IL. Rt. 154. When I arrived the truck was nearly submerged. Only the top of the cab was visible. Looking around I could not find any reason for the crash. I had to wait for the tow company to remove the truck to see its registration and test it's steering. The truck had no obvious damage other that water damage from going into the pond.

I drove to Pinckneyville's hospital. The doctor was already working with the driver. The doctor handed me a read out on the driver's blood. The blood showed high levels of THC.

I am not a pharmacist but THC is an active ingredient in marijuana. Evidently the THC is the ingredient that makes the marijuana smoker feel "high." Whenever I would discover THC in the blood, the person would be charged with DUI. (Driving Under the Influence)

A DUI (Driving Under the Influence) arrest for an automobile operator is difficult. The driver must ordinarily pay a large fine, go to alcohol classes, wait out a period of suspension before driving again, and pay a reinstatement fee to the state of Illinois. All the listed problems with the government do not end the drivers cost. The DUI convicted driver must pay his lawyer and deal with his insurance company for at least three years of heightened premiums. But for the DUI truck driver it is worse still. Chances are that driver will never drive a Commercial Motor Vehicle (Big Truck) again. The insurance costs to any trucking company wanting to employ such a driver would be prohibitive of employing him/her.

As I wrote this young man his reports, I am not sure he knew his truck driving career was over. The driver's wife was present and wanted to know what was going to happen. I explained the DUI and the court procedures. At this point she asked if I thought he would be able to return to truck driving. I told her the truth on how it would be hard for a company to insure him.

The truck drive's wife began to weep. She claimed to have no knowledge of his marijuana smoking.

I felt a great deal of grief for this woman. Assuming she was telling me the truth of her lack of knowledge of her husband's marijuana habit, she was the real victim here. She and her child (she had a small child) were going to go from middle class citizens to destitute literally overnight. Her husband had made the choice (to smoke cannabis) that would likely forever alter his family.

I left the hospital glad I could protect the innocent citizens of Illinois from an impaired truck driver. Perhaps I had saved a person's life by getting this man off the road. On the other hand, by doing my job I had forever altered this young wife and child's standard of living. I thought no wonder so many cops turn to alcohol. There is just no winning on cases like this one!

CHAPTER 13
ACCUSED OF RACISM

Racial tensions today are at a high not seen since the 1960's. Ferguson Missouri lit the fuse when officer Darin Wilson (a Caucasian) shot Michael Brown (an African American). Since that incident, a group called "Black Lives Matter" has come to the forefront of what appears to be a new type of civil rights movement. The period between the 1960 race riots and today's new civil rights movement was when I served as a State Trooper. While the period I worked was far more peaceful than the 1960's or today, no officer wants to be accused of racism. When an officer is accused of racism (and even if later found innocent), the stigma of racism attaches to that officer.

One accusation was minor and quickly passed. I stopped an oriental lady's son speeding some twenty miles per hour over the speed limit in a construction zone. The oriental lady was the front seat passenger and claimed I singled her son out because he was oriental. I was on videotape and so I pointed out to her she was being racist for accusing me of racism when I was just doing my job. I told her that she surely knew her son was traveling over the 45 miles per hour speed zone; so to accuse me of being a racist was in fact a racist act on her part. The lady calmed down and apologized.

The second case was much more involved and could have been more serious. I was at home eating my lunch, midway into my shift, when the phone rang. My State Police headquarters was calling. I was told a Master Sergeant was behind a car coming Northbound from Marion Illinois on I57 and the car was traveling 95 miles per hour. I was told I was to go to the interstate and stop the car as it got to West Frankfort.

Not wanting to leave my lunch, I asked why the Master Sergeant did not make the stop himself. I was told the Master Sergeant was using the car for his personal business (only Master Sergeants and above in rank could do this). I was told the Master Sergeant had his teenage daughter in the car and did not want to make the stop.

I got to the interstate and located the car that I had been phoned about. I locked my radar on the car and it showed the driver was speeding by only one mile per hour above the speed limit. The driver was going 66 miles per hour in a 65 mile per hour zone.

I did not want to make the stop for the driver doing one mile per hour above the limit but figured I would do so and let the Master Sergeant write the ticket for the 95 miles per hour speed he had observed. I turned on my overhead lights and got the car to stop just North of the West Frankfort exit.

I walked forward to the offender's car and began my usual spiel. "Hello, I'm Trooper John Gossett and the reason I stopped you is..." When I reached the word "is" the driver, an African American male held up his hand to motion for me to stop talking. I stopped to hear what he had to say and he replied, "You stopped me because I'm black."

It was nighttime, somewhere around 9:00 P.M. So I looked across the interstate and asked, "what race is the driver in that car that is coming toward us."

"How would I know it's dark," my suspect replied.

Exactly I pointed out. It is dark and you cannot tell the race of any driver. So I did not pick you out by race.

With my point made on racism, I told driver that my boss had told me to pull his car over due to his excessive speed of 95 miles per hour. I explained my boss was now stopped in his own squad car and was behind us.

The driver was upset and said my boss was a liar. Since my boss was the one who clocked the guy speeding, I had him talk to the suspect. This proved to be a mistake, as it created a shouting match. The driver was shouting my boss was a blanking liar and the boss was saying the driver was a lying.

I had already gotten the driver's license of suspect and as he and the Master Sergeant yelled at each other I performed a driver's license check on my suspect. I had dispatch check this driver in all 50 states. The driver was valid in Missouri, where he presently lived, but was suspended from his previous state of residence, Alabama.

At that time, a suspension in any state meant you were driving while suspended and subject to arrest. I told my suspect to quit arguing. I explained I would be issuing a warning for the speed and a citation for his suspension. This left the Master Sergeant out of the case and I could deal with it directly.

I got the suspect handcuffed and inventoried his car; as I had to tow it. As I took stock of what the suspect had in his car, I found an open whiskey bottle under the seat. I would charge the driver later for unlawful transportation of alcohol.

My Master Sergeant decided he could not let the excessive speed go. He wrote the suspect a speeding citation from Williamson County (near Marion, Illinois) for the 95 miles per hour speed. My Master Sergeants actions were fine with me as it put his case in a different county court and he could testify to what I could not confirm; which was the excessive speed.

Several days after the incident I became aware of a letter sent to the Benton, Illinois mayor. A group of African American attorneys were writing to say my actions were racist. The Benton mayor had no jurisdiction, as both my Master Sergeant and I were with the Illinois State Police. Then Benton mayor forwarded the letter to the Illinois State police.

I spoke to the issue with my Lieutenant. I said the case should be directed to the Master Sergeant as he initiated the incident and was present for the entire stop. Now the State Police may or may not have been fond of me but they clearly would want to protect their Master Sergeant. The case was closed shortly after the Master Sergeant spoke with the higher command.

I do not feel anything about the stop was racist. Assuming the Master Sergeant saw the car traveling at the 95 miles per hour speed, nothing was done that was illegal, immoral, or even impolite. It sure is bad to be called a racist though. There should be a charge to arrest someone on who calls "racism" when there is none!

CHAPTER 14
ANSWER THAT RADIO!

Radio communication was the lifeline to police in my era. Whenever an officer went on a traffic stop, he would radio in the location of the stop, the license number of the suspect's vehicle, and the vehicle's description. The tele communicator would then tell the officer if the registration was clear. A clear response from the tele communicator meant that registration was not on a wanted car or one involved in an armed robbery or murder, etc. Later, when electronic communication equipment improved, a tele communicator would often tell the officer what type of car the registration went to. For example the officer might be told the registration was to be on a 1995 Chevrolet. If that registration plate was on a Buick, it increased the odds something was amiss and warned the officer to be aware.

Once the officer made the stop, he had five minutes to report back to the tele communicator. If the officer failed to call in within the five minute time table, the tele communicator would begin to call out the officer's car number. In Illinois the State Police had 22 districts. The first part of the car number was the district number. For example, I was from district 13 so the first part of my number was 13. The second part of the number was your rank in district. Car 1 belonged to the Captain. Car 2 belonged to the Lieutenant. Cars 3 through 9 belonged to the Master Sergeants. Cars 10 through 16 belonged to the sergeants. Numbers beyond 16 went to the Troopers and were not assigned in any particular way.

On each shift the Troopers would learn their fellow workers car numbers and patrols. If something went down you knew who was involved and generally where they were. Management tended to rove around so a Trooper would have to pay special attention to know their location.

On the night of my story, I was gassing my squad car up in West City, Illinois. Near Johnston City, Illinois on I57 I could hear car 13-3 making a motorist assist. When 13-3 gave his location and the registration of the car, he was told the system was running slow. Running slow meant the officer is going up blind as to the car being a suspect's vehicle. Often the computer system would not be completely down but it would take minutes instead of seconds to get the clear signal.

Shortly after officer 13-3 should have got out of his vehicle I hear that the car is a stolen vehicle. I am paying my gas bill and am running to my car. I am 12 miles away from 13-3 but may very well be the closest back up car.

Officer 13-3 is not answering post broadcast. Now post's tele communicators are broadcasting 13-3 location and car number and the fact he is not answering his radio and has a stolen car. Post is asking for certain cars to give their location. I am the closest car.

Now I'm running "hot". I have my lights and siren on and am traveling 130 plus miles per hour. Post asks me every minute my ETA (estimated time of arrival). Post is also still calling out 13-3's number and location.

I arrive and 13-3 and a Johnston City cop are sitting in 13-3's car. The suspect is finishing tightening up his last lug nut on his stolen car wheel. The suspect's girlfriend is anxiously waiting his finishing the tire change (they had a flat tire and had to stop).

I walk past my boss's car and get behind the suspect. I get him by the shoulders so he can't swing the tire tool and hit me. I explain that he is under arrest and to drop the tire tool. The suspect does as told and I handcuff him.

Police are to answer within 5 minutes of a stop. I have missed this 5 minute rule a few times. Usually you get involved in doing something and forget to call in. Most of the time you recover in time that little damage is done. This stop was a case where all kinds of harm could have occurred.

The suspect could have driven off. The suspect could have hit the officers with a tire iron. I could have crashed my car racing to the scene.

This wake up call convinced me to change my policing tactics. I always carried a portable radio before this but from that point on listened better. I paid more attention to a system running slow message. System running slow meant you might well be in danger and not know it.

Well no harm was done and in the end and the suspect was arrested. Perhaps the moral for the suspect is to pick a car to steal with better tires. And for my boss 13-3 the moral is "answer that radio."

CHAPTER 15
ARRESTING A FAMOUS PERSON

Americans love superheroes. We love Superman, Batman, Green Lantern, and many more. Perhaps the one superhero that gets most overlooked is the guy in the red suit that flies around in a sleigh, pulled by eight tiny reindeer. This guy, regardless of the weather, delivers toys all over the world in a single night. This guy, as you have figured out, is Santa Claus. Perhaps you have never thought of Santa as a superhero till today. As hard as it is to admit, I arrested Santa Claus.

One late evening in December, I was in West Frankfort, Illinois. I got behind a green jeep as it headed east toward Thompsonville, Illinois. The green jeep was going over and back on the center line that divided lanes of traffic. The jeep was getting into the oncoming traffics lane. I activated my overhead lights and got the jeeps driver to stop. I went forward to the jeep and there was my superhero... Santa Claus.

Yes he was dressed in a red suit with black boots. Even his cheeks were a rosy red from having lipstick rubbed into his skin. All this Santa lacked was his beard. Evidently he had removed the beard prior to driving his jeep.

I recognized Santa as a man who had once helped me roof a house. I called him by his real name and got his drivers license. I explained to the man he was driving all over the road. I also explained that I smelled alcohol on his breath.

The pretend Santa explained he had been to a Christmas party for underprivileged kids. He said his motorcycle group gives away toys every Christmas to the motorcycle group's children and underprivileged kids. He said this year he had been chosen to be Santa.

I explained I'm all for free toys to underprivileged kids but felt the need to know where he (Santa) was that made the drinking necessary. My Santa said the party was held at a West Frankfort bar. Santa admitted to having a few after handing out the gifts.

Evidently Santa had drunk far more than a few beers. Santa was soused. When I got his from the jeep he was falling down drunk. I placed Santa under arrest for DUI. I handcuffed him and put him in my squad car.

Another officer from a different agency arrived. The second officer was struggling with my decision to arrest Santa. He seemed more inclined to get him a ride home.

I explained no one gets a break from me on DUI. Santa suit or otherwise, this kind of behavior is not permissible. This Santa's action of driving, while DUI, was going to lead to more underprivileged kids when he kills their parents by driving.

Following the towing of Santa's jeep, I transported him to the Franklin County jail. I got Santa in and then the inmates realized Santa had been arrested. The hoots and hollers from the inmates were pervasive throughout the jail. The inmates were very upset that Santa had been arrested so close to Christmas.

Santa was later convicted and lost his driver's license. I suppose the next time I see him around Christmas he will be driving his sleigh pulled by eight tiny reindeer. I know that he can't legally drive that jeep.

CHAPTER 16
ARRESTING ICEBOX

I grew up in a small town of 10,000 people. There were six separate grade schools in my community but only one junior high and one high school. This meant that in grade school you (a student) did not know all the kids of the town. After arriving at junior high, you learned of many kids you had not previously known. This is a story of one of the kids I met at junior high called 'Icebox."

I was in seventh grade when I met Icebox. Icebox had been detained several times and would have been some two or three grades older than me. Icebox would always wear mirrored sunglasses (it was his trademark). Icebox was from a bad family and was a troublemaker. I recall the gym coach telling us what kind of gym clothes to buy. The required clothes were a pair white shorts and a white t-shirt with the logo Central Junior High printed on the front. The coach almost apologized for the cost of the clothes since we would only wear them for two years before graduating to high school. I recall he looked at Icebox and said Icebox had gotten a good deal when he purchased his gym clothes as he had now gotten four years out of them. I did not see much of Icebox as he skipped school far more often than he attended. When Icebox was around, he always was threatening and bullying other younger students. Icebox's one friend, a boy named Freddie, was as old and mean as he was. Luckily for all of us younger kids Freddie liked to skip school with Icebox so we rarely dealt with either boy.

After junior high, I ran with Icebox on a couple of occasions. From what I could see, Icebox's life consisted of drugs, alcohol, and fighting. As time went on, I heard Icebox had been sent to prison. I suppose the last time I saw Icebox before I arrested him was when I was 16 years of age.

Somewhere around my 32, birthday I was working as a state policeman and was at the Franklin County jail. A county Deputy handed me a warrant sheet. The Deputy wanted me to see if I knew anyone on the sheet. The Deputy said if I did know someone please lighten the county's work load by picking the subject up and bring them to jail.

I had never had a warrant sheet before. My method of finding those wanted for warrants was to accidentally stop the wanted persons vehicle and then find out they were wanted by running their driver's license data through a computer. Looking at the sheet I recognized a few names. The one that stood out was Icebox's real name.

I never cared for Icebox due to his tendency to bully people. Fortunately I had grown up and he no longer dwarfed me in size. While I was not afraid of him and did not hate him, I knew if I saw him I would have to arrest him. I also expected a big fight when I attempted the arrest. Icebox wasn't all bluff, he would fight.

I was on Il Rt 149 in West Frankfort Illinois when I observed a man crossing the highway to go to a movie rental store. The fellow was wearing mirrored sunglasses. Yes it was Icebox.

I stopped the car and went toward Icebox. I informed him he was under arrest and spun him around and handcuffed him. Surprisingly I got no problems out of Icebox.

In my car, when we were headed to jail, I looked at Icebox and asked why he didn't fight me. Icebox said he had a bad wreck the previous week and had severely damaged his nose. Icebox said he was too sore to fight or he would have. Icebox said he would have fought to the death as he had sworn he would never return to prison. Icebox wanted to know why the officer that had taken care of his wreck had not arrested him. He wanted to know why all the other officers who had seen him had not attempted to arrest him.

I explained to Icebox I had no idea why others had not arrested him. I took his sunglasses at the jail and realized he was missing part of his nose bridge. As I locked Icebox up, the other inmates picked up word Icebox had been jailed. The other inmates began to yell "Icebox is in the cooler" and "Icebox is on ice." Icebox began to curse and yell threats to those who taunted him.

Icebox went back to prison on this occasion and I heard once more later. I read a few years ago where Icebox died. I think what could have been done to prevent his incarceration? Seems like no one knows!

CHAPTER 17
ARRESTING SHOE PIPE

From the time I was born, my father's World War Two buddies would come by the house and see my dad. Most of my father's friends had taken jobs in the coal mines of Southern Illinois. Coal miners and WW2 people tended to have nicknames that were used instead of real names. One such fellow was Shoe Pipe. I have no idea where he got such a nick name. The man was a character. I recall he was loud and full of curse words. He was always involved in union (United Mine Workers) business. He was in fights on a regular basis but I don't recall of hearing him winning any fights.

The original Shoe Pipe had two sons; the oldest became a coal miner like his father before him and took on the nick name Shoe Pipe too. The rest of this story is about the son who will simply be called Shoe Pipe.

I had been a coal miner for six years before becoming a State Police officer. I took a leave of absence from the State of Illinois in 1994 and went back to working at the coal mine for six months. When I returned to the mine, I received a phone call from Shoe Pipe. Shoe Pipe had received several DUI's and did not have a driver's license. He requested I give him a ride to and from work. This Shoe Pipe, was like his father before him, in that he was loud and obnoxious. I put up with Shoe Pipe for a week of riding together. Then I was able to get on a different shift and no longer had to ride with him to work. Six months after agreeing to ride with Shoe Pipe, I returned to the State Police.

One evening I pulled into the Huck's convenience store in West Frankfort. There was Shoe Pipe filling up a yellow Buick with gas. Shoe Pipe had another notorious fellow nicknamed Tex with him. I walked up to Shoe Pipe and told him he needed to call his father for a ride. I said; "Shoe Pipe you and I both know you do not have a driver's license. I cannot arrest you here because you are on private property filling your gas tank. If you attempt to drive and I see you I will put you in jail. Is that clear?"

Shoe Pipe always called everyone "Pard". Shoe Pipe says "sure Pard" and goes to a pay phone and appears to me to be calling for a valid driver to drive him off. So I went on my way.

A half an hour later I see the same yellow Buick that Shoe Pipe had been filling with gas coming up a side street to Il Rt 149 in West Frankfort. I look in and sure enough it's Shoe Pipe behind the wheel.

I activate my overhead lights and get the Buick to stop. I really thought Shoe Pipe would make a run for it but he must have thought he could talk me out of arresting him.

Shoe Pipe got out and said; "what is the problem Pard."

I said Shoe Pipe you are under arrest for driving while revoked. "I gave you a chance at Huck's to avoid this."

Shoe Pipe said; "No you did not Pard. You never said you would arrest me."

About this time Tex spoke up. Tex said "yes he did Shoe Pipe I heard him say he would arrest you."

Shoe Pipe went to jail. He begged for me to let him go the whole way there. I said :" Shoe Pipe you know I gave you every opportunity to avoid this... have a good night in jail!"

CHAPTER 18
ARRESTING THE DEPUTY'S

There is an unwritten rule in law enforcement that you don't arrest another cop or his/her family member. If the crime was not serious, like minor speeding in which there was no accident involved, I normally gave strong verbal warnings or warning citations (Note; I did this for the general public as well). When the crime was DUI, I did not go along with the unwritten rule. I was hated by other officers for my policy but I felt if justice were to be served, it must be blind. That is to say all people are treated equally. This is a story of the Deputy's son.

I was patrolling Benton Illinois in the early hours of the morning (probably around 1 A.M.) when I observed a pickup truck going over the center lane line on North Main in Benton, Illinois. I stopped the driver and he was very intoxicated. I had just finished the field sobriety test when a County Deputy approached. The Deputy told me that I had another deputy's son stopped. The Deputy said this young man regularly drove drunk and had been given breaks in the past.

I don't think the arriving deputy wanted the drunk set free. My feeling was that he was aware of my reputation and wanted this guy gotten off the road. The Deputy's speech was ambiguous but I felt he did this to protect himself in case anyone asked what he had said to me.

I replied that if this guy had gotten breaks before today was the end of his breaks. I handcuffed the young man and took him to jail.

Once at jail, I saw the young man's dad arrive. The arriving father never said word one to me as I completed the arrest of his son.

The father made sure the son got bail and took him home after the arrest.

I worked with the father (who was a Deputy Sheriff) for ten more years or so. The man was a professional, as I could not tell he ever treated me differently after the arrest than before it .

The good part of this story was the father got his son assistance for his alcoholism. I had heard the son was able to turn his life around. This story goes to show often consequences (DUI arrest) have results. Without my arrest this young man would have continued to drink and drive. The end result of the young man continuing to drink and drive would likely have been his own death or the death of another innocent person. I just wish they would have all worked out so well!

CHAPTER 19
BEER ON MY HAT

A policeman wants to keep things under control. Surprises are never supposed to happen. Surprises will get an officer hurt or injured. Here is a case where I was surprised but it only left me a little embarrassed and smelling like a beer.

I was on IL Rt. 14 just West of Christopher, Illinois around midnight. I was following an old Chevrolet with Georgia registration. The Georgia registration on this old stretch of state highway was unusual. On the interstate, a Georgia registration would be common but here it had my attention. I could see the car had three occupants. The occupants were moving around as I followed the car. Movement like I was seeing often means the occupants are hiding drugs or other illegal items. The car was going over the center lane marker line.

When I turned on my overhead lights the Chevrolet pulled onto a small side road. The fields on both sides of this lane were full of tall rows of corn. I walked to the car and spoke with the driver. I asked for a license and the driver provided a Georgia driver's license. The driver was old enough to drink and smelled of alcohol. I explained he was going over the center line and asked what brought him to Southern Illinois from Georgia.

The driver said he grew up in Christopher, Illinois. The driver said he was out drinking with his cousins, who were his passengers.

The driver was sober so I explained I had a reason to search his car due to the furtive movements I had observed when stopping him. The driver said we don't have anything so go ahead and search.

I sent the driver to the front of the car and had him place his hands on the hood. I got drivers licenses from the cars two passengers. I put my hat in the middle of the front seat between myself and the front seat passenger. As I was reaching under the driver's side front seat, the front seat passenger suddenly said," F*** you copper." He reached to the area between the passenger seat and the passenger door and brought out a bag of marijuana and threw it out his window into the corn. Now he grabs a beer from the same area and pours it on my hat.

I had already jumped back, when the kid yelled and threw the marijuana out the window. I was thinking I was going to be shot. So now that I am back from the car, I can't stop the kid as he empties a most of a 12 ounce beer on my smoky bear hat.

I was upset but intended to make a lawful arrest for criminal damage to state supported property. I ran to the passenger side to bring the young man out. The kid scoots across the front seat of the Chevy, he exits the car from the driver's side, and runs into the corn. I am faced with chasing the fleeing passenger or staying with the two occupants and the car. I make the right choice and pick the car.

I issued the two young men that remained with the car citations. The driver got a citation for lane usage and illegal transportation of alcohol. The back seat passenger got a citation for illegal transportation of alcohol. I decided only the fleeing passenger would be cited for the cannabis.

I have the kid's identification that ran into the corn. I even have his picture. I can get a warrant to arrest him with later but I want to make this arrest myself. That night I pray I will get an opportunity to make the arrest. I decide to hold onto my report one more day. (I normally always turned my reports in as they were generated. We had a two day window to get the reports submitted and I decided here to go the second day)

The following day I call my suspects home and speak with his mother. I explain I want her son to call me and turn himself in to me. The mother promises to tell her son I called but openly doubts he will turn himself in. She describes her son as a dangerous boy and asks me to be careful around him.

The following night I immediately return to Christopher as I intend to hunt for my suspect. It is about five in the afternoon when I pull onto a parking lot used by the rougher young people in Christopher. Amazingly there sits the Chevrolet from the last night. In the Chevrolet, in the passenger front seat, is my suspect.

I pull in quickly and position my car at an angel where the suspect must flee to my side of my own car. I put my bumper to where the suspect can barely open the door of the Chevy. The suspect is trying to get out but has trouble due to my front bumper not allowing him to open the door all the way open.

I grab the suspect and he does not resist further. I handcuff him and take him to jail. I don't have to do a second report, I just add tonight's activities to yesterday's activities.

My suspect spent the night in jail on a felony charge of destruction of state property. I knew the states attorney would plead it down as it wasn't a serious crime. The states attorney did this young man a big favor. The kid got all charges dropped by joining the Armed Forces. I was glad it ended this way so the young man could get some structure in his life.

My hat sure smelled like a beer though!

CHAPTER 20
BIG GIRL IN A CAR CRASH

Americans are becoming bigger and bigger people. I can personally attest to that fact and need to lose a few pounds myself. Extra weight, especially a lot of extra weight, can cause a person huge (pardon the pun) problems. Chairs don't work anymore. Airplane seats are too small. For first responders to accidents, extra pounds really make our job tougher. For example, getting a 120 pound person from a burning car versus getting a 500 pound person from a burning car is totally different. In fact, in the case just given, the heavy persons has an increased chance of dying because the first responder probably cannot physically remove them from a burning car. This story is a case of dealing with a very heavy person.

It was nighttime on a crisp fall evening. I get a radio dispatch to a car crashing between two bridges on Il Rt 13 just East of Marion, Illinois. I get to the crash site and there is a small creek that runs across Il Rt 13 and the road builders have installed two bridges to cross it. Il Rt 13 is a four lane roadway at the bridge site. The eastbound bridge has two lanes of traffic that it handles and the westbound bridge has two lanes of traffic it handles. The car driver has driven between both bridges and shot about 30 feet into the creek. To get to the car we, first responders, must slowly walk down a concrete incline sideways. The center concrete section between the bridges appears to me to be on a 15% grade. (for readers who do not know this is a very steep incline)

I get to the bottom of the incline and discover a very heavy female driver (estimated to weigh 300 pounds) and an average size male passenger. Both the male and female are very drunk. The air bags of the car probably saved their lives. The impact of the cars speed and the 30 foot drop has destroyed the vehicles front end. The drunk people are dazed from impact and must be put on gurneys for transport to the local hospital.

The male presents a slight problem due to the incline but we get him loaded and transported by ambulance. The female is a different problem due to her weight. The ambulance people enlist the firemen and eventually we get her from the car and get her on a gurney. We now have two ambulance men and three firefighters and myself to get her up the incline. I'm thinking it over and don't believe we have the human power necessary to get this lady up the incline and in the ambulance. So I stop everybody and at the bottom of the incline a conference is held.

I explain I don't think using people to haul this lady up the incline is a wise idea. I want to use the cable of a tow truck that is on the scene to hook onto the gurney and pull the lady to the top of the incline. I explain we could simply guide the gurney to the top and let the tow truck wench do the work.

The lead fireman says Chanel 3 news is on the scene and he doesn't think my idea would look very professional to the public.

I explain using the tow truck wench is better than ruining our backs or even worse dropping the lady down the embankment because we can't take her weight.

A decision is made due to the influence of the fireman and we are bringing her up with human power. I was so disgusted with the decision I said I was going to the front of the gurney so as to try to save my back.

Up we came from the bottom of the incline to the top. All six of us on the gurney were straining to the max to accomplish this task. I looked and the fireman who was insisting on using human power was in the last position on the gurney and was getting the most weight. This fireman was a big guy but was at the end of his strength.

We got the lady loaded and got her to Herrin Hospital. Within minutes of my arrival there she was up and around as if she had not been injured. I gave the woman a DUI and went on my way.

About a year later, I'm off duty and am shopping with my wife at Sam's club in Marion, Illinois. I see a guy on a cane barely able to get around. I'm feeling sorry for the guy who obviously has serious back issues, when he turns around. Yep it's my fireman buddy from the incline wreck involving the big girl.

I go up and greet my fireman buddy and ask what caused his condition. He replies "don't you remember that big girl we hauled up the incline. I haven't had a good day with my back since. I've had a back operation which hasn't worked and I'm told I'm on disability for life."

I reply yes I remember her. I still wish we had used the tow truck wench.

My fireman buddy now agrees with me. I sure hope he gets better.

CHAPTER 21
BUSES

When you ask most people about transportation, they most often seem to think of trucks, cars, planes, and trains. The reality is that many Americans use buses. Some buses are used for cross country travel with a company like Greyhound. Other buses are owned and operated by tour companies that make the trip a virtual vacation while in route to a destination. In either case, these buses need to be inspected from time to time to make sure they are safe for people to use. Fortunately bus wrecks are rare. Bus wrecks are so rare the Illinois State Police seldom needed an officer to inspect them. So when a bus wreck occurred an officer would be dispatched from Springfield, Illinois (our headquarters) to perform the inspection.

The drive time from Springfield to say Cairo, Illinois is about three and a half hours. Someone in Springfield finally had the good sense to say that an officer from Southern Illinois needed to be trained to handle such a rare occurrence as a bus wreck.

Why I was chosen to become the Southern Illinois bus inspector is beyond me. I did not want the job and told my superiors that I did not want this position. I was told to shut up and head to Peoria, Illinois for a week of bus training.

The bus training went well. I enjoyed learning about buses. I discovered buses were much different from trucks and cars. Bus brake systems and frames are much different than that of a truck (which surprised me). Obviously the bus escape system through the windows of the bus is different than any other form of transportation I had seen. What really stood out in my training was a warning not to inspect buses going down the highway. If an officer stopped a bus going down the highway and found a serious bus condition, all the passengers would then be stranded while the bus was repaired. Obviously stranded passengers would generate complaints against the department. Susses should be inspected at points of destination when the passengers had disembarked.

Finding a place to inspect buses in my little district posed a problem since there was no place to disembark bus passengers. The only place I could inspect buses anyway near my district was in Metropolis, Illinois at the gambling casino. To get permission to go there was problematic. Metropolis was out of my district and any inspections I generated there would go to the next district's total. My superiors did not want the next district to get the credit for the inspections done there by me. On the other hand, if I could not get 13 inspections per year I lost my bus inspectors certification.

I informed my lieutenant of my need to do 13 bus inspections at Metropolis, Illinois. I only received the promise that time would be provided at a later date to do these inspections. In the meantime, I was given a small trailer to pull behind my squad car. The trailer contained bus ramps to elevate the bus for an inspection.

A little over a year later the event arrived. A bus hit a fireman on I57 near Benton, Illinois. The fireman was killed and the bus had to be inspected. The lieutenant phoned me to do the inspection. I told him I had not been given time to do my 13 inspections and therefore was no longer a certified inspector.

The lieutenant went into a rage. I explained his being angry did not change the situation. A certified inspector was needed and I wasn't the person.

A bus inspector was sent from Springfield and I assisted him in inspecting the bus.

The lieutenant sent me to bus recertification school. I got recertified. The lieutenant swore this situation would never occur again.

I got recertified. I informed the lieutenant that I need to go to Metropolis, Illinois to do 13 buses. I was told time would be allotted later.

You (the reader) guessed it Deja vu. A bus wreck happened an inspector is needed. I get the call. I have not done 13 inspections and thus lost my certification. The lieutenant is pissed.

It ended here. The district took my little bus trailer away. I was never recertified. All future bus crashes received an inspector from Springfield. The little endeavor to have a Southern Illinois bus inspector went down in flames. If only I could have had time to do 13 buses in Metropolis!

CHAPTER 22
BY THE BOOK BOB

Every organization small or large has a" by the book person." You have seen them; they have a certain personality that drives them. Their personality is such that they must follow the rules.

The State police had a book of rules (operations manual) for each officer. The book was red and had about four inches of printed material inside it. The book is divided into sections. For example, one section was on how to wear a uniform. This section dealt with the wearing of the hat, hat band, and hat medal. Then it dealt with the shirt, shirt medals, and buttons. Another example is the section dealt with weapons. What type of ammo was permissible, when to use the weapon, when and how to clean the weapon. A third example might deal with hostage situations, what to do on arrival, when to negotiate, etc. As you can easily see, the book covered almost any situation an officer could come upon as well as his/her dress. No one person could know this manual well enough to live by it. In the case the officer screwed up, the book was brought out and some section was cited as the officer's failure to live up to the manual.

Some of the State Police leadership tended to take the manual to heart more than others. One such man had the first name of "Bob." Bob would see you at the courthouse and be upset if you were wearing boots. It did not matter that the boots were issued from the quartermaster; Bob wanted you in the shiny shoes. Bob would point out that only the shiny shoes were listed in the manual for use in court. For his constant attention to the book (manual), the Troops referred to Bob as "By The Book Bob."

Bob was in charge of the tactical response team. Bob's squad decided to pay a trick on Bob. The team members removed Bob's front license plate from his squad car. They took the plate some 300 yards down a hill and put some brush near it to camouflage the numbers on the plate which read 13-7. The members then had a shooting contest using their long range AR-15 rifles. The team members got close but deliberately did not shoot Bob's license plate.

Bob was looking on in disgust. He could not believe his team members were shooting so poorly. Finally Bob picked up his Ar-15 and announced he would show the other members the proper way to shoot. Bob hit the target squarely with three successive shots. Bob looked up to the awe and approval of his team members. They were cheering Bob on.

Finally a member said, "Bob let us go see what you have hit." As the team got close to the license plate they could hear Bob, who was with them, begin to cuss. Bob discovered he had shot his own license plate three times in the middle.

Bob was upset. He had all his men get out the proper form, from the manual, and write an explanation as to what had occurred. Bob vowed vengeance on the culprit who had removed his license plate and made it a target.

The men had discussed the possibility of Bob going to the manual to get a sworn form to try to make them tell him who the ringleader of this conspiracy was. So each man had a prepared statement which they wrote on the form. The statement said, "we do not know why our Master Sergeant shot his own license plate."

Bob was furious but was unable to get to the bottom of who led in the setting him up to shoot his own license plate. My guess is "By The Book Bob" filled out a false form saying his license plate had been damaged by road debris on the highway while he was driving. If this were to be true, shouldn't the Troops have changed his name to "Not By The Book Bob?"

CHAPTER 23
CAN I SMOKE IN YOUR CAR?

I am not a smoker. I did smoke as a teenager but got out of the habit when I was about 19 years old. At the time of this story, the general public was unaware of the dangers of secondhand smoke. I did not let anyone smoke in my squad car, because as a nonsmoker, I did not like the smell.

It was 1987 and I was in rural Monroe County. I had a pickup order on a suspended driver's license with an attached warrant to boot. (We actually use to go to homes of those with suspended license and took the physical document from the driver.) The warrant meant if I discovered the person I was to take the license off of, I was to handcuff him and bring him to the county jail for lockup. The warrant meant a judge had found reason to have that person placed under arrest. An officer must obey a warrant, so no officer digression is allowed.

The warrant listed the suspect as Jim Jones with a height of 6'2" tall and 200 pounds with brown eyes. I went to the location listed on the warrant and driver's license. I went to the rear door of the home. Experience had taught me to go to the rear door. The people in the homes expect cops at the front door and friends to the rear door. When I knocked, I stood to the side of the door so my uniform would not be visible. Then when the people inside ask who it was knocking, I would always reply with my first name "John." Usually those inside would know some person whose name was John and would open the door. This procedure worked hundreds of times and rarely was I left outside and not be able to speak with the homes occupants.

This day went as usual with a man answering the door. I looked and he was about 6'2", weighed 200 pounds, and had brown eyes. I said, "Hello, I suppose you are Jim Jones."

No he replies back, "I'm Jack Jones."

I have been fooled a time or two by relatives. They know their brother's or cousin's dates of birth and unfortunately look like them. When I asked where Jim was I got an "I don't know answer."

I felt like I had probable cause to make this arrest. I was at the correct address. I had a guy that matched the height, weight, and hair color of my suspect. The man I was speaking to was not leveling me with his supposed brother's whereabouts. I handcuffed the man and took him to the county lockup.

At the jail, I was doing the paperwork necessary to jail my suspect when in comes the Sheriff of the County. The Sheriff greets me and then looks at my suspect and says "Hi Jack, how are you?"

I ask the Sheriff, "are you sure this is Jack and not Jim."

The Sheriff assures me he has known the Jones boys since they were born and this is in fact Jack.

I tore up my paperwork. I release Jack from handcuffs. I tell him how sorry I was to arrest him as I thought he was his brother. I offer to take him home.

Jack is a little miffed. He had insisted I had the wrong guy all along and I did not believe him. I took him from his house in handcuffs. In spite of it all, Jack said he would take a ride back home.

I'm driving Jack home. Jack smokes and looks at me and says, "can I smoke in your car?" I reply, by all means please smoke." I figured it was the least I could do for Jack after ruining his day.

CHAPTER 24
CAPTAIN O' CAPTAIN

There is a saying that says, "Be careful who you offend on the way up the ladder of success." I have found this saying true. Never make enemies unless absolutely necessary. The people you make as enemies may someday have control over you and it may not go well. This is my story of a difficult Captain I encountered early in my career as a policeman.

In 1987 I was hired by the Illinois Secretary of State Police and entered the Illinois State Police Academy. Upon completion of the academy, I was assigned to E. St. Louis Illinois, which is about a hundred miles from my home in West Frankfort, Illinois. I fell under a particularly difficult Captain.

I had previously been an underground coal miner and had purchased a home in West Frankfort, Illinois. I had put $14,000 in my home and it literally represented all the money I possessed. I had placed the home on the market to sell but the area I lived in was economically depressed and the home was not selling. The Director of the Secretary of State Police had given me permission to drive a squad car back and forth to E. St Louis each day if I would make at least two traffic stops coming and two returning from my base of operations. I was fulfilling the Directors mandate by making the required traffic stops.

The Captain did not get along well with the Director and was upset that the Director had gone around him to make the decision to allow me to drive to E. St. Louis. Thus the Captain disliked me for being able to get around his control.

Every week I would be called into his office for a "you can't continue to drive to E. St Louis speech." The speech always pointed to the fact the captain had to move from where he grew up to where he now lived for the sake of the Department. He would say he moved and by George I would have to move too!

I would point out that my house was in fact up for sale. I would say I was doing my best to get moved to St. Clair County as he (the Captain) wanted. I would show how I was leading the department in activity. Finally I would remind the Captain, that his superior the Director had given me permission to drive.

When I made the last point about the Director giving me permission to drive the Captain would get enraged. He would say I'm going to put an end to this. There are people above the Director who can force his hand and I'm going to them. You will see.

Evidently the Captain did have clout above the Director because the Director came to E. St. Louis, Illinois to see me. The Director said I was in fact leading the department in activity but he had to order me to move. The date was set as June 1st 1988 for me to move or be terminated.

Fortunately I was able to transfer to the Illinois Commerce Commission Police on June 1, 1988. The problem was solved but I never forgot the Captains difficult attitude towards me.

Fast forward eight years and I am now an Illinois State Trooper. It is 1995 and I am in the (FTO) field training program. I have to ride with another Trooper until he deems me able to be by myself. The other Trooper is in effect my boss. It is late in the evening and I am in Jefferson County on Il Rt 37 South of Mt. Vernon Illinois. I see an old beat up pickup truck pulling a beat up trailer. The trailer lacks lights and registration.

I get the old truck and trailer stopped and then I go forward to speak to the driver. Oh yes! It's my favorite former Captain.

I act professionally and ask the Captain for his license. The Captain is worried. Since the Secretary of State Police work with registration, a citation from me would mean a short time off without pay for him. He says, "John you do recognize me don't you." I replied "Why yes Captain I recognize you."

I go back to my squad car. My FTO officer is concerned. He asks what I intend to do. I explain this Captain has violated two laws and deserves two citations. My FTO forbids it. I explain I would write any normal person the citations and I want to write these. Again I'm denied permission to write the citations. The FTO doesn't want to get into what he called a pissing match with the Secretary of State police.

I went toe to toe with the FTO but got nowhere. I sat in the car and wrote on a tablet. I think I made the Captain believe he was getting citations which would have given him time off his job. Then I went forward and lectured the good Captain on the danger he caused the public for not having lights on his trailer. I also spoke to him concerning registration laws which he enforced but was now disregarding.

It was a good feeling to have the upper hand. My message to the Captain is this: "Captain o Captain be careful who you abuse with your power because you never know when those bad actions will later have unintended consequences."

CHAPTER 25
CIGARETTES

Many people in our country like to smoke cigarettes. Smoking is a particularly bad habit as it has been linked to cancer for years. Regardless of the risk, people, like my own father, just seem to enjoy it and continue to smoke.

Government's response to smoking is very pragmatic. Cigarette smoking is a great way to raise taxes. Sin taxes, which include both alcohol and tobacco, have been around for years. The rate of taxation is high, as these sin taxes seldom affect the general public. Those who like to smoke and drink just seem to overlook the tax and pay up without any real complaint. So here we have a win/win for the government: a lot of tax money with few complaints about the tax.

With tobacco the rate of taxation is largely related to a state's geography. Southern states with tobacco farmers tend to have very low rates of taxes on cigarettes whereas northern states, which have no tobacco farmers, have high rates of taxes. My state of Illinois is a northern state with no tobacco farmers (its growing season is too short for tobacco) and thus has a high tobacco tax. Illinois is surrounded by Kentucky and Missouri which both have very low taxes on tobacco. The result of Illinois being so near tobacco states is that smuggling is a big deal. Cigarettes bought in Missouri or Kentucky cost half of what cigarettes bought in Illinois do.

Tobacco is shipped to Illinois in unmarked packages. Each pack is given a stamp, which is purchased through the Illinois Department of Revenue (our taxation department). To see if a pack of cigarettes is properly stamped, our revenue people show up at a store and pull a pack of cigarettes from the shelf. The pack should show a stamp with the word "Illinois" on it. If the pack lacks a stamp, the cigarettes are probably from a stolen semitrailer that never made it to the tax stamp center. If the stamp reads Kentucky, then the retailer has probably went into Kentucky and bought cigarettes to resell for a higher profit and avoid Illinois cigarette taxes. In either case the retailer is in big trouble for avoiding Illinois tax laws.

As bad as retail tax evasion is, the state of Illinois real problem is individuals who travel out of state into a tobacco state and buy out of state cigarettes. In Illinois, during my career as a Trooper, an individual could legally buy one carton of cigarettes out of state and transport it into Illinois.

I was patrolling near Shawneetown, Illinois around the year 2000. I was about ten miles from the Kentucky border. I pulled over a truck and as I walked to the truck I could see multiple cartons of cigarettes on the truck driver's passenger seat. I popped open a carton and it had Kentucky stamps on the packs. A second carton was opened and the Kentucky stamp was also on each pack. The driver admitted purchasing 24 cartons of cigarettes for himself, his sister, and his brother-in-law in Kentucky. He said he knew it was wrong but with the price being half of what Illinois purchased cigarettes cost he decided to take the risk. The driver said his brother-in-law and sister had put up the money for their part of his purchase.

I immediately seized the cigarettes and gave the truck driver a receipt for his cigarettes. I explained if he could prove he legally owned the cigarettes, they would be returned.

The driver remarked he had never seen the "government ever return anything."

I knew the driver was correct as he was never going to see these cigarettes again. I could just see this poor guy telling his sister and brother-in-law that he had no cigarettes to show for taking their money. I could see him showing them my receipt for the cigarettes and trying to explain that he did not steal their money. I could see this guy with serious family issues.

I took the driver before a judge who released him on his signature. This was a kindness on the part of the Judge as the driver had committed a felony.

I heard the driver was convicted and released. The Judge gave the 24 cartons of cigarettes to the Sheriff for the inmates to smoke (yes this was a long time ago). I heard the inmates of Gallatin County were smoking to the heart's content for a couple of weeks. I heard they would finish one cigarette and then light a new one off the one just smoked. Rumor was there was a haze of cigarette smoke around the jail.

As for the driver of the truck, I am sure he could say the statement "smoking is bad for you" certainly proved true.

CHAPTER 26
COP RUNS OFF FROM DUI

People often do stupid things. In major cases, you hear of the man who rapes a woman and then to cover it up kills her. As bad as the rape is, the killing of the victim is far more heinous. The penalty for the murder can be a lifetime in jail or even capital punishment. The punishment for the rape would be 12 years. Criminals often don't think through the possible end result of their crimes till they have been caught and cannot stop what is going to happen to them. This is a story of a cop who got a DUI and fled the scene.

Somewhere around 1997, I was on patrol in Williamson County. I was driving Eastbound on Il Rt 13 and was approaching IL Rt 148. The car ahead of me was swerving back and forth over the lane lines. I activated my emergency lights and got the car pulled over.

The driver, I had stopped, immediately informed me he was a police officer from a town in the Southeast part of Illinois. He went as far as to display a badge. While I cannot read this man's mind, I suppose he thought being a police officer meant that I was going to overlook his driving while drunk.

Since the driver reeked of the odor of beer, I took him through the field sobriety test. The driver failed badly and was soon handcuffed and in my car. I had his driver's license in my possession and had the tele communicator at my post in Duquoin, Illinois put his name through a driver's license check.

Now the cop under arrest could not be stupid person and get a job as a policeman. He has had to pass some type of intelligence test to get his job. He knows, I know who he is and where he lives.

Further I have his driver's license in my possession. Finally remember he is handcuffed. For the cop to run off at this point in my stop is stupid behavior.

I go up to search his car and he manages to slip the handcuffs from behind his back to the front of his body. He releases the seat belt I have placed on him. Then he opens my squad car door and flees into a cornfield. He spends three hours on the run. County dispatch was getting calls of this guy going to farmhouses and trying to get the farmers to cut the handcuffs off. Finally three hours later the cop's girlfriend brings him to me at the county courthouse. He is still handcuffed, though he did manage to bend them.

The cop now wants to take the breath test.

I told him the breath test was a refusal when he fled.

The cop loses his job. He is found guilty of DUI and fleeing. He gets to buy me a new pair of handcuffs for bending them while fleeing.

The cop would have possibly have won his court case if he had not fled the scene of his arrest. He might have kept his job (back in those days) even if he had been found guilty. He certainly would not have had to purchase me a new set of handcuffs.

Yep, that cop sure displayed some stupid behavior!

CHAPTER 27
CRAZIEST COP I EVER MET

Crazy can be defined many ways. Some crazy people are dangerous. Some crazy people hear voices. While I have encountered both dangerous people and people who hear voices, the crazy I speak of in this story is crazy funny. This is my story of Lan, the craziest cop I ever met.

One day while working at a truck weigh scale in Maryville, Illinois, I left my cell phone unattended. The Master Sergeant on duty quickly returned my phone. The Master Sergeant informed me that when working with Lan, I should keep my cell phone with me at all times. I asked why Lan would be a threat if he got hold of my cell phone and the Master Sergeant said Lan would do all sorts of mischief if he got hold of anyone's cell phone. The Master Sergeant said he had been a victim of Lan. The Master Sergeant went on to tell me this story.

He master Sergeant said he had left his phone unattended in Lan's presence and Lan had gotten a hold of the phone without his knowledge. The Master Sergeant said he always phones his wife by using his speed dial. Lan had changed the number of the Master Sergeant's wife on his speed dial to the number of another Trooper. The Master Sergeant phoned the listing for his wife and this other Trooper answers. The Sergeant was surprised to hear the Trooper; as he knew voice on the phone. Thinking his wife must be with the Trooper, he asked to speak with his wife. The Trooper responded he had no idea where the Master Sergeants wife was.

Now the Master Sergeant was thinking his wife and the Trooper he was speaking with must be having an affair. The Trooper was denying knowledge of the wife's whereabouts and yet was answering her phone (remember this is not the Master Sergeant's wife's phone but the Trooper is answering his own number on his own phone). The Master Sergeant said he got very angry at the Troopers denial of knowing where his wife was. He said he began to threaten the Trooper with bodily harm. The Master Sergeant says, " if you are not with my wife why are you using her phone?"

The Trooper who had been phoned by the Master Sergeant tells him (the Master Sergeant) he is losing his mind. The Trooper said that he still had no idea where the Master Sergeant's wife was but the number the Master Sergeant was calling was his (the Troopers) phone. The Trooper tells the Master Sergeant that he will overlook his crazy behavior this time but if he calls back he will put in a formal complaint. The Trooper then slams the phone down.

The Master Sergeant said that the Trooper claiming the phone he had called was the Troopers own phone got his attention. The Master Sergeant said he had used his speed dial for so long he did not actually know his own wife's phone number. When he got his wife's number from another source, the Master Sergeant realized his speed dial had been altered by Lan.

The Master Sergeant said he had to phone the Trooper he had offended back and apologize. He said everyone in the district laughed at him for a while but a friend of his got far worse treatment from Lan. He told me a different Master Sergeant got transferred to his District in Southern Illinois from Chicago. The newly arrived Master Sergeant bought a double wide modular home from a Dealer I will call "Dream Homes."

Lan had heard that the new Master Sergeant had bought the home and promptly phoned him. Lan claimed to work for Dream Homes and said the home the Master Sergeant had purchased could have and electrical defect in the wiring. Lan said to speed up the inspection on the home the Master Sergeant should put all the furniture in the middle of each room so the wall sockets would be easily accessible. Lan said that Dream Homes understood that all this work of moving the furniture to the middle of each room would be an inconvenience and would buy the Master Sergeant and his wife a fine diner at Red Lobster for their efforts. Lan tells the Master Sergeant coupons for his free diner will arrive by U. S. mail.

A couple of weeks after Lan's call, still has the Master Sergeant living with all his furniture in the middle of each room. The inspector, who was supposed to inspect the modular, has not arrived. Even the coupons for the Red Lobster dinner have not come in the mail.

The Master Sergeant is livid. He phones Dream Homes. He demands to know where the electrical inspector is at who was supposed to inspect his home. He tells of living with all his furniture in the middle of each room while awaiting the inspector. Finally, he says, "where are my Red Lobster coupons that were to come in the mail."

The Dream Homes manager is dumbfounded. He cannot answer this man's rants. The manager finally tells the Master Sergeant he must be the victim of a bad practical joke.

The story would be funny if it just ended here, but it doesn't. Lan was unable for years to be promoted even though he was exceedingly bright. Lan's big break came when he got shot in the leg at the Range by a Master Sergeant. (Note: everyone said it was an accident as the Master Sergeant claimed he thought the gun was empty as he started cleaning it). The leg wound put Lan on crutches for a period of time but failed to dash his spirit. The shooting did seem to change his promotional ratings. Perhaps the Master Sergeant who shot Lan felt responsible and wanted to make up for his shooting him. In any event, the last I heard of Lan he was moving up the chain of command. I wonder if he is as crazy as ever?

CHAPTER 28
CRAZY HILL

Young people often make big mistakes in their lives. Some mistakes can be so bad as to impact them for years into their adulthood. My mother always said that young people would turn out fine once their over "crazy hill." My mother's words are where the title of this story came from. My own journey to get over crazy hill almost cost me a chance to be a Trooper for the Illinois State Police.

When I was from 14 to 18 years old, I was a very foolish young man. Two of my serious vices were drinking liquor and stealing.

At around 14 years old, I found a bar in a little town of Freeman Spur called Pistol's place. The bar was about eight miles west of my hometown. The bar got its name from the previous owner who wore a pistol and a holster as he served drinks. The place had brown tar paper siding and was in the middle of a 400 person town. No sign was up and you simply had to know where the business was or you would drive past it. At night, a single light bulb on the porch burned indicating the place was open. The bar, in my time, was operated by Pistol's daughter. Age was not a problem. If you could afford the drinks they were served with no questions asked.

I got rides to Pistol's bar from older high-schoolers until I got my own motorcycle at 15 years of age. I had a job and spent all my money at the bar. Later when I turned 16, I got a car and used it as transportation to Pistol's bar. Needless to say I was a teenage drunk. Most nights I would consume from 6 to 8 drinks.

At 16 years of age, I got a job at Jim Martin's Carpet World in West Frankfort, Illinois. I recall starting at $1.60 per hour as a cleanup boy. I swept the floors and washed windows. I was the highest paid working kid in high school. As time went on, I got more responsibility in the store. I was mixing paint and helping to install carpet. My wages did not go up with the new responsibility and my other friends were now earning more than I was with their jobs.

I went to the manager, who was the owner's son. I asked for a raise and was promised one. When I did not receive it, I went back to the manager and asked what was up. The manager said the raise was not allowed by his father. I really did not believe the manager. He probably decided on his own to not give the raise.

The problem with the manager telling me no to my raise was twofold. First, as I stated I did not believe him, and second, he was regularly taking cash from the register. I thought (and to this day still think) the manager was stealing cash register money. He obviously did not have to account for the removed money as he just took it without even leaving notes as to the amounts he was removing

When I received my paycheck on Friday, I would cash it myself from the cash register. I took the money I was entitled to on the check and also took the amount the manager had previously agreed to as my raise. I was never caught, as the manager never knew how much money he was supposed to have in the cash register. The managers own stealing covered up my stealing.

By the time I was in my 20's I had become a Christian. I never stole from an employer again. I also quit all heavy drinking of alcoholic liquor.

I was a coal miner in my 20's and became a policeman for the Illinois Secretary of State Police at 31 years of age. I worked as a policeman for the Secretary of State and the Illinois Commerce Commission till age 39. My past crazy behavior of drinking and stealing had never come up in my employment interviews.

When I decided to become an Illinois State Trooper, I was given a form that asked me to list all my past violations of the law. The form listed driving while intoxicated and then gave the following possibilities. One time, two times, five times, ten times, fifty times. Stealing from an employer read the same way.

I raised my hand and asked, "is this form asking about the last ten years or a lifetime." The trooper giving the test probably did not know the answer so he shouted out like a drill instructor, "just answer the question."

I knew that polygraphs were sometimes given recruits for the Illinois State Police. I also knew I did not want to tell a lie. So I picked fifty times of DUI and fifty times as stealing from my employer.

I had passed the written exam and had the qualifications to be a Trooper, so the next step was to meet the psychiatrist. As I walked in I could see the psychiatrist was unhappy. He said "we have never hired someone with a background of so many DUI's and thefts from an employer. Why should we hire you?"

I explained my youthful stupidity. I told them how I had had a clear change in my life in my 20's and had not driven DUI or stolen since I was 18 years old. The psychiatrist said he would consider my application after all, since I had cleared up my answers.

The psychiatrist then said, " I have one last question. If you could be reincarnated into any animal what would it be?"

Without hesitation I said I would become a Polar bear.

The psychiatrist then jumps up almost into my face and says, "do you want to be big and bad and scare people? Do you want to tear people apart?"

I replied, "No I want to be like the polar bear and be able to do the backstroke while swimming."

A big grin appeared on the psychiatrist's face. He said, "You passed, now get out of here!"

CHAPTER 29
DOGS

I want to start this story out by saying I'm a dog lover. I have owned dogs most of my life. I still appreciate my daughters' dogs. With that said, I don't like dogs that bite and don't intend to be bit if at all possible. The following is a story of my several dealing with dogs that would bite.

I was sent to look for stolen cars at a junk yard in rural Monroe County in 1987. Illinois had a law where Secretary of State Police can look at all junk yard records without a search warrant. As an officer, you take down the Vehicle Identification Numbers (VIN) of a few cars on the lot. Then compare those VIN's with the titles or junking certificates, the junk yard has in its files. If no title or junking certificate is located, the VIN in checked on the national data base of the FBI to see if the car is stolen.

As I arrived at the junkyard, I could see the driveway was a one lane road. The junkyard was so full of cars the owner had lined both side of the road with junk cars. The owner was pulling the tires and wheels off of all the cars and so the vehicles were setting on the ground.

I drove down the one lane road about a quarter mile and then had to stop for junk cars ahead of me. I walked another quarter mile to the junk yard shop. It was probably 10 A.M. and I expected the place to be opened but the door was locked and no one was around.

I looked and off to my right was the residence of the junk yard owner. I watched as the back door opened and a big man let two dogs out. One dog was a Spits and the other a German Shepherd. The dogs were on alert as they were released and were obviously coming to bite me. The only thing that slowed the dogs down was the cars that were on the ground prohibited them from coming straight to me.

I pulled my revolver and waited. The Spits was quicker of the two dos and as it went for my ankle, I shot it in the head. I hit it in the forehead right between the eyes. The poor dog died instantly. The Shepherd heard the gunshot and ran off.

A female and the male, who had let the dogs out, came quickly out of the house. The female was very upset at the male for releasing the dogs. The male was mad at me for shooting the dog.

My opinion is that the male knew I was there and decided to let his dogs corner me. The female knew that the male had let the dogs out on me. So she blamed him for the loss of her dog.

I phoned post and told of shooting the dog. A shooting team was dispatched. The team measured the dogs distance from me. They took my gun and counted the number of shots taken. They took pictures of the dead dog.

I knew I had a date with the shooing inquiry board so I investigated the junk yard owners. I discovered the junk yard owner's dogs had bitten three people. They had bitten a neighbor, a county deputy, and a passerby on a bicycle. I put all this in a report and got two statements from those bitten. My case was solid so I forgot it.

Unfortunately, I had to back to the same junk yard. The same woman I had dealt with over her dog was crying when I contacted her. I tried to be nice but had a hard time understanding why she would be crying over my killing her dog some six months earlier.

The lady said she was not crying over the dog I had killed but over her Shepherd. She said her Shepherd had been out with her son on the road that is a half mile from the house. She said that a car had passed her son and the Shepherd. She said the driver stopped his car on the road and then deliberately backed over her Shepherd.

I felt sorry for this woman but I knew the history of the dogs. I knew of three people bitten by her dogs and how they were going to bite me. So I said, "I'm sorry, that's really hard to believe." I was sorry for her and it was hard to believe someone went that far to kill her dog. I did not say what I felt, which was the dog was a danger and the world was a better place.

CHAPTER 30
DUI TRIAL IN FRANKLIN COUNTY

Every police officer despises going to trial. No matter how well the case is prepared, there is always some weak point in any arrest. Something the officer wishes he had done better. Something he wishes he had asked a particular question and failed to. Some piece of evidence that could have been handled better or taken instead of left. Good defense attorneys know this and attempt to discredit the arresting officer. The defense attorney attempts to make a "boob" of the arresting officer who has attempted to be fair with the accused.

The case here involved my being called to a small community in Franklin County in the late evening hours. A car crash had occurred on the main street of this community. I arrived and discovered the vehicle had crashed into the only tree on this community's main street. The driver was bleeding badly from his mouth. He had bitten his tongue so badly was nearly severed. As the suspect spoke the smell of beer was strong and blood was gushing from his mouth. The suspect was so intoxicated he was staggering.

I asked the suspect to please quit talking and keep the pressure on his tongue with a towel someone had provided him. Every time the suspect attempted to speak to me arterial blood would come streaming from his mouth. The EMTs soon arrived with the ambulance and took the suspect to the Franklin County Hospital.

After towing the wrecked car and securing the empty beer bottles, I headed to the Frankin County Hospital to work with the suspect. When I arrived, the suspects tongue had been sown back on by the attending emergency room physician.

I read the suspect his "warning to motorist." This is a legal document that tells the suspect that he can refuse to give blood, breath, or urine to me but the penalties (In terms of suspension time) for refusing to do so are greater than doing so. Of course refusing has the advantage of making it harder for police to secure a conviction on a person who is over the intoxication limit. As I read the document, my suspect began to act like he was asleep.

When I finished the reading of the warning to motorist, I asked my suspect if he would give me a blood sample. Still acting asleep I got no response. I verbally warned the suspect that if he continued to play asleep the law allowed me to take a blood sample without his consent. At which time the suspect quit playing asleep, raised up, and spoke very incoherently and in a nasty tone some undecipherable words.

I told the suspect to nod yes or no to the question as to if he would voluntarily donate me a blood sample. He shook his head violently no he would not give me a voluntary sample of blood and again spoke incoherently. I recorded both his nodding no and his incoherent speech in my arrest report.

Surprisingly this case went to trial. In Franklin County on trial days, those incarcerated in jail are transported to the county courthouse which is some three blocks away. The prisoners are in orange jumpsuits and are handcuffed. These unfortunate souls then have to wait their turn to see the judge until after those with attorneys get their trial. I suppose the idea is inmates have nothing better to do than sit in court while those with attorneys are paring $300.00 per hour for an attorney. The judges give those paying an attorney a break and let them go first.

In any event the courtroom was packed with those awaiting their cases and prisoners. The defense attorney was attempting to discredit my arrest of her client and asked me to state what her client said when he was asked to give blood. I explained that he violently shook his head no to the request and spoke incoherently. The attorney looks at the judge and says your honor please make this officer tell the jury exactly what my client said. I looked at the judge and said are you sure you want me to answer this question. The judge assured me I must answer it.

I answered "Owemetontonrondonfn". No this is not a typo, my answer was as unintelligible as the suspects was on the night of his arrest. The prisoners in the courtroom were now hooting and hollering and laughing. The judge was laughing so hard he had tears running down his face. The judge was banging his gavel trying to bring order to the court but was unsuccessful; as he was laughing. The suspect was looking at his attorney like you stupid idiot what have you done. Five minutes later order was finally restored. The defense attorney had violated an elementary principle of "don't ask questions which you don't know the answer to."

Needless to say five minutes after I had begun to be cross examined by the defense I had secured a victory. The defendant had been found guilty. Although I had been pummeled by attorneys on other occasions, I got the better of this one today.

CHAPTER 31
FEDERAL COURT

As a State policeman, I spent a good deal of time in Illinois Circuit Courts. In Illinois every county has a circuit court, usually at the county seat. The courthouse is usually noisy. Often prisoners are there from the county jail, dressed in their orange jumpsuits, and usually hoping to qualify for release on recognizance (their signature). The proceedings are seldom watched closely. Business grinds on for two or three hours at a time. Sometimes, and I do mean sometimes, a full formal trial takes place. As a rule, a deal is worked out in a plea agreement so the real trial never takes place. With the Federal system, the courthouse scene is quite different. The judge sits on what appears to be a 6 to 7 foot tall bench. The bench is very high to indicate power. The courtroom is dead silent unless the judge directs someone to speak. Everyone's attention is on the matter before the judge. I had only one experience before a Federal Judge and this is it.

The story begins in Marion, Illinois on a hot summer afternoon. I observed a driver without a seat belt at Il Rt 37 and Main Street. I pulled the car over in a movie rental store parking lot. The driver attempted to get into the store before I got to him. I ordered him back to his car. I asked for his driver's license. The man said he did not have his license with him so I did as I always did in this situation, I handed him a small pad and pen from my front pocket. I told him to write his name, date of birth, and address on the paper. The man did as I requested. I looked him up in the driver's license data system and found he had a valid license. I then wrote him a citation based on the information he had provided.

I recall the man wanted to talk. The man was worried that since he was on federal probation this citation was really bad for him. I said he would have to tell his probation officer of the citation but I felt that this would not amount to a big deal as it was only a seat belt citation. The man was obviously not calmed by my statement that this was not a big deal.

Several months go by and I get a phone call from an assistant federal prosecutor of the Southern District of Illinois, Federal courthouse in Benton, Illinois. The prosecutor wants to know about my stop of the man for the seat belt violation. After locating my copy of the citation, I explained my actions. The prosecutor wanted to know where I got the address from on the citation. I explained my giving the man my pad and pen and he provided the address himself.

The federal prosecutor then surprised me. He said drive yourself to the location on your citation and then phone me back. I did not argue and did as told. I found the address to be a parking lot behind a bank. There was not any structure on the lot where a person could reside.

I phoned the federal prosecutor and explained the address was obviously not correct as there was no structure for housing; as the address belonged to a bank parking lot.

The prosecutor said she was aware of the fact the lot was a bank parking lot. She said she wanted me to know that fact. She said I would be receiving a federal summon to appear at the Benton Federal courthouse. I would have to testify to the fact I had been given a bogus address.

I showed up in court and see the man I had arrested in Marion for the seat belt violation. He has a woman with him who is every bit of nine months pregnant.

A hearing is held and the man is found to have violated his parole. He begs the judge for leniency saying that his girlfriend is nine months pregnant and needs him to be present for the birth of their child. The Judge isn't buying the story. The man gets a year and a day back in prison for giving me a false address.

I am amazed. People lie to me on a regular basis and even when I charge them with obstructing justice in state courts, the charge is usually dropped (even though it's a felony). Here a guy gets a year and a day for lying. Wow!

After my own case was adjudicated, I decided to watch the next case. A man, who had been an assistant local fire chief, had already been convicted on child pornography. Today was the man's sentencing hearing. In state court, I knew he would have drawn about a ten year sentence. This judge handed down a 30 year sentence. The defendant was already in his fifties and was begging the judge to reconsider, as this amounted to a life sentence for him. The judge responded,"you should have thought of that before you did the crime."

Being in Federal Court taught me a lesson... stay out of federal courts as a defendant!

CHAPTER 32
FIGHTING A CANADIAN

Let me start this story by saying I have nothing against the fine citizens of Canada. Truthfully though, I have had far more negative incidents with Canadian truck drivers than I have from Mexican truck drivers. I say this as I have had frequent contact with both. I finally chalked it up to the Canadians don't get enough sunlight. Living in the frigid North, they spend far more time indoors and get less sunlight. Perhaps that is the reason they are often on edge (just kidding but something is different).

On the night in question an Old Sergeant came to the scale to work with me. Sarge was on his last week as a policeman and was looking for a safe place to work. He had ordered a driver to pull a truck into the scale house parking lot. Sarge was waiting for his stopped truck driver to come inside the scale as I went out the scale house door to meet my driver outside.

My truck was a tanker and I had climbed on top of the trailer to see if the lids of the trailer were properly fastened on this hazardous material load. While on top of the trailer, I heard the truck weigh inspector come over a Public Address system at the scale and scream 10-33. 10-33 is an emergency code and I knew something bad was happening in the scale house and the truck weigh inspector was wanting me to come inside immediately. I slid down the tankers ladder and ran into the scale house. The old Sergeant was wrestling with a much younger man. The fight appeared to be a draw as neither man was winning.

I grabbed the younger man and threw him over a table in the scale house. I got him handcuffed. I asked Sarge what was going on. Sarge said this guy went off on him over a warning ticket.

I told Sarge to get his paperwork together and I would transport this guy to jail for obstructing a police officer. I told Sarge I would transport him since he was more upset with him than me. Sarge was to follow me to the jail as soon as he could.

I put the suspect in the car and started driving to the county jail. As we went toward the jail, the driver informed me he was a Canadian and was a member of the Royal Canadian Army. He said he could bust my handcuffs off anytime he chose. I looked at my Canadian passenger and asked if he would just please wear the handcuffs till we reached the jail.

Now I had never seen anyone break a pair of handcuffs and this was the first time anyone had ever threatened to do so. I did not think this guy could actually break a pair of handcuffs but I really did not want to find out. My mind wandered to having to fight this crazy guy while driving and I really did not like the idea.

After telling the suspect to just wear the handcuffs, he started the whole thing over of being a Royal Canadian army vet who could break my handcuffs. So it went over and over again as we drove along.

When I finally reached the jail and had opened the sally port door (once in the sally port the prisoners are locked into the jail), I told the Canadian just do what you have to do with those handcuffs. He began straining with all his might to break my cuffs. His face became red and arms tense but he did not break my handcuffs. He then looks at me and says " ah for your sake I will just wear the handcuffs."

This man could not admit defeat. Guess he needed more sunlight.

CHAPTER 33
FINDING OUT HOW MUCH I'M WORTH

Did you ever wonder how much your worth? I don't mean what your assets are. I mean how much would a person pay to meet you. Political dinners often show me how much a politician is worth. I have heard of political dinners of $10,000 per plate. I've heard of politicians paid $400,000 for a speech. Big politicians are evidently worth a lot of money to see and hear. I'm evidently not that important, but I can give you a pretty precise value on what it is worth to meet me. I'm worth somewhere between $75.00 and $350.00. This story is how I came to know my worth.

I was driving Southbound on I57 and was nearing a construction zone when I looked in my rear view mirror and saw a very fast approaching tan Buick. I used my rearward facing radar to lock on the coming car. The speed was near 90 miles per hour in a 65 miles per hour zone.

I was driving a Chevrolet SUV in those days and was often confused for vehicles other than a squad car. I was told by one offender that I drove an ambulance. Another time I was told I had a highway maintainer car. Evidently the female driver of the Buick thought my vehicle was not a squad car either as she blew by me.

I was going to stop the Buick before the construction zone but to do would have put everyone in harm's way. Too often officers do stop cars before a construction zone and then get hit by oncoming traffic. The traffic cannot see the last arrow pointing traffic to a single lane because the squad car blocks visibility of the arrow. I had a good friend killed when he stopped a car at a lane change arrow so I was well aware of the danger.

As I followed the lady in her Buick, I realized she was going way too fast for a construction zone. I hit my front radar and it indicated the Buick was going 70 miles per hour in a 45 miles per hour zone.

In Illinois at that time a speeding citation was $75.00. Speeding in a construction zone was far more serious. The fine for speeding in a construction zone was $350.00.

After both the Buick and my squad car exited the construction zone, I hit my overhead lights. The Buick's driver pulled to the side of the road. I went forward to meet the driver.

I explained to the driver that I had stopped her for speeding and got her information. The lady was from Kentucky and was very flirty. She did not seem at all bothered by my having stopped her.

I went to my squad car and wrote this lady a citation for speeding in a construction zone. I went back to the Buick and began to explain the citation. The lady stopped me from talking and said she had always wanted to meet an Illinois State Trooper. She said she knew her fine would be $75.00 but it was worth every penny to meet me.

I explained to this lady that normal citations are $75.00 but speeding in a construction zone is $375.00. The lady's face contorted at the revelation that she owed the great state of Illinois $375.00. At this point she gave me a cussing.

So there you have it. For $75.00 this lady thought I was worth meeting. For $375.00 I was only worth a cussing.

CHAPTER 34
FOOLING AROUND WITH THE OTHER POLICE

In the late 1980's computers were put into the police stations. The first computer I saw was a DOS (Disk Operated System). A large book sat next to the computer and it was necessary to look up whatever function you wanted to do in the book before attempting to get the computer to do the job requested. Any missed period or mark that varied from the books example would make the computer fail its requested job. Frustration accompanied every job attempted.

Somewhere around 1995 my platoon's office received one of the very up-to-date computers. This system allowed even non-computer people like me some ability to produce reports and graphs. The graphs were a new phenomenon to me. With a little work, I was able to produce a pie graph. The pie graph is a round circle (like a pie your mother baked) in which you can show percentages of what the pie represents. For example, if officer A does 50% of the arrest in his group of 5 officers, the pie would be cut in half by a line and officer A would be shown responsible for half the work of the platoon.

The Sergeant of our platoon was very computer knowledgeable and often produced good results using his computer. He was ahead of his time and we in the platoon all knew of his computer savvy. I had never seen the Sergeant do a computer graph but was convinced if I produced one everyone in the platoon would believe he did it.

I produced a pretend graph. On it I listed all five officers in the platoon. I gave each a percentage of the pie graph. The one officer I was attempting to mess with received a 1% of the total arrest. (While the officer was not the highest worker in the platoon, he certainly deserved a much higher rating than 1% and I'm sure he knew it). On the bottom of the graph I wrote, "Officer John ***** your activity is entirely too low. Please come to my office to discuss your work performance." I signed it with the Sergeant's name. I then placed the graph in Officer John's mailbox.

Naturally John was ready to accept the Sergeants challenge listed on the pie graph. John knew his performance was well above 1% and believed he was being unfairly singled out. So john went to see the Sergeant. When he entered the Sergeants office, John was in a huff and had the pie graph in his hand.

I could not see or hear what happened in the Sergeant's office. I suspect john went in demanding the pie graph be fixed to show his actual activity. I'm also reasonably sure the Sergeant was asking where John got the pie graph that showed him (the Sergeant) as the author.

John looked a little sheepish after learning the Sergeant had not singled him out and the pie graph was a fake. Old Sarge wanted to know who had produced the graph. As for me, I was lying low to avoid detection.

After about a week, I fessed up to the Sergeant and John. The weeks delay in confessing allowed everyone to calm down. All was well and everyone enjoyed the pie graph joke. I should add that old Sarge did forbid any further false pie graphs.

CHAPTER 35
GETTING PAST THE MEAN NURSE

Police officers and nurses have a normally tight relationship. We understand they have a tough job to do and they understand that we have a tough job as well. Nurses nearly always get a break on minor traffic violations and in return they often go out of their way to assist officers who must work with suspects that have been hospitalized. It often happens that police and nurses become lovers and mates as a result of bonds formed as part of this unique relationship. If nurses, particularly emergency room nurses, are attacked the police are their defense. With all this as a background, I can say I have met only one difficult nurse and this is the story.

I was called to Il Rt 1 near Carmi, Illinois to investigate a truck tractor trailer versus car crash. This was way out of my traditional patrol boundary by this time in my career. It seems the truck specialist, who worked in the Carmi Illinois State Police office, was on vacation so I had to replace him.

I drove an hour and arrived to see a truck tractor driver had been passing in a no passing zone going up a hill. Some poor woman had topped the hill from the opposite direction and been hit nearly head on. The woman had tried to veer her car off to the passenger side of the road but the truck driver was in a skid and slid into her vehicle. The lady and two of her three children had been killed.

A check of the truck yielded no issues with the truck. The drivers steering and brakes all worked well. This meant the crash was a result of driver error or in this case driver recklessness.

I drove to the hospital in Carmi to speak with the driver. My plan was to get a statement from the driver as to why he was passing in a no passing zone going up a hill. I suppose there might be a legitimate reason for this maneuver. Perhaps the driver was passing a unit that deliberately sped up which would leave the driver with the choice of backing off or speeding up. Perhaps this driver made the wrong choice and sped up only to his horror to find a car in his path. If this were true then the police need to find the other errant driver of the vehicle being passed. As you can see from the possible situation I just explained, it is very important to speak directly with the driver and the earlier the better before he has time to concoct an untrue story to cover his criminality.

I went to the nurse's station and asked for the room number of the driver involved in the crash on Il Rt 1. This is southern Illinois and my question would not have yielded a response of "which crash on Il Rt 1." With so few people in this part of the state there are few car crashes and the nurses would immediately know who I was looking for. The nurse who appeared to be in charge said the man I was looking for could not be seen.

I explained I really need to speak to the driver and asked if the doctor had prohibited my seeing this man. The mean little nurse said no but I still could not see him.

Well police don't run hospitals. Without permission from the staff, I felt like I could not go to the suspect's room. I intended to put the fact I was refused the right to see the suspect in my report and let it go. I sat down in an area of the hospital and began to do what paperwork I could do.

I had noticed a guy that appeared to be agitated walking around the hospital coming right next to my location. Pretty soon a different nurse comes to me. She tells me that this walking gentleman is in fact the driver I am looking for. I ask if she minds me talking to him. This nurse says "have at it as long as you stay out of his room."

Well I got my answers! Guy admitted to driving too fast to try to make up time so as to be at a delivery on time.

Sure was glad to get around the mean nurse. I never saw her again... glad I didn't... what a jerk.

CHAPTER 36
GUN PLAY

In my 25 years plus of actual police work, I seldom drew my pistol. I suppose I drew it between five and ten times during my career. My thoughts were never draw your pistol until you feel in extreme danger. I also knew that if I did draw my pistol I fully intended to use it. By God's grace I never fired on anyone or was fired upon. This is a story where it was a very close call on whether I killed a man or not.

In my career I have done hundreds of drunk drivers. The unwritten rule is most drunks go to the same bar nightly. These drunks have a back way home and use it exclusively. The back way is designed to stay clear of law enforcement and they know this way home so well that being inebriated doesn't affect their ability to find their homes. People who do not follow the above rule tend to come to law enforcement's attention far quicker than those who do follow it. On the night of my story I had a drunk that did not follow the above rule.

I was on I57 in the wee hours of the morning when I observed a pickup that was weaving over the center line and then back into the proper lane. When drunks do this, it appears as if they are in slow motion and has a different look from someone fighting drowsiness who usually jerks the car back into the proper lane.

I got the truck stopped and asked for a driver's license and proof of insurance. The driver, who smelled of alcohol, removed his license from his wallet and then went to get his insurance card which was in the glove box. As the glove box opened, I could see a pistol inside it. The driver was reaching for the pistol instead of his insurance card.

I quickly pulled my own pistol and stuck in the back of the drivers head. I said if you grab that gun I will kill you.

The driver sat still and I opened his door and pulled him out of the truck onto the ground. I replaced my pistol and handcuffed him. I collected his pistol and towed his truck.

At jail I charged the driver with DUI and illegal possession of a firearm.

The driver decided to taunt me. He said "you were bluffing about shooting me. You couldn't have done it."

I explained to the drunken idiot that yes I fully intended to kill him if he grabbed his gun. I asked what choice I had except letting him shoot me.

My statement that I would have killed him sobered my drunk up. He appeared as if some of his color had drained from his face and was now subdued. He said yes he understood I would have had to kill him.

Drunks often do very stupid things. Perhaps this guy intended to scare me by pulling a gun. I can only say I am really glad I did not have to kill him. That would have affected a lot of people. It would have affected his family and mine. I would have needed more therapy that I already do. Oops! There goes that police humor my wife tells me not to use!

CHAPTER 37
HAZMAT SPILL FROM ILLINOIS TO ARKANSAS

The great state of Illinois has specially trained Troopers for almost any emergency that might develop. We have scuba divers who go underwater if needed. We have accident reconstructionists who figure out exactly what happened in a car crash involving the death of person. We also have personnel trained in how to deal with hazardous material. I was chosen to be a Hazmat officer.

Hazardous material is any substance that poses an unreasonable risk to any person. Hazardous material classifications have been around since the civil war. During that war, trains carried munitions and were a hazard to those in close proximity. The placarding system was developed to warn people of the danger the train held and to let specialist know what the train carried without getting near it. We still use placards today. For example a class 1 placard means the truck carries explosives; while a class 3 means the truck carries flammables. After designing eight placards, the hazardous materials experts designed a class 9 placard. The class 9 is no less dangerous than those that precede it but covers any material not covered in the previous 8 classes.

I was working at the I57 Northbound scale in Williamson County one day when I observed a class 9 placarded truck come upon the scale. The truck tractor unit was spilling liquid out the rear of the unit as it came upon the scale. I had the unit come to the rear of the scale. I also shut the scale down so as to prohibit any other person from possibly stopping at the scale and becoming contaminated.

I had the driver bring the shipping paper to me. This paper shows exactly what the material being hauled is, where it came from, and where it is going. The material being hauled came from a steel mill in Arkansas. The material was going to Chicago, Illinois to an incinerator. The material itself contained nickel, and other heavy metals.

The hazardous material was in a huge triple layered plastic bag. To a layman it would be like triple bagging your trash but here it was 80,000 pounds of trash. The bag had been cut open and someone had attempted to reseal it with duct tape. These triple layered bags are never intended to be unsealed. The huge bags are handled by equipment at the shipping site.

I asked the trucker what had happened as shippers don't ship bags of hazmat that have been cut open. The trucker gave me this story.

The trucker said he had waited three hours in line with his truck to get this load. Once loaded, the steel mill has a scale, and so he weighed his truck. Unfortunately the truck was overweight. The driver said he thought of unloading the whole load and then getting in line and asking for a lighter load. (This would have been the proper thing to do). The driver said he did not wish to wait another three hours for another load so he had an idea. The driver said he had a hazardous material suit in his truck with a breathing apparatus. He said he donned the suit and took out his trusty pocket knife and cut into the plastic bag covering the hazmat. The driver said he took off about 1500 lbs of hazardous material. He said he threw the hazardous material aside at the shipper' business. He said he felt the shipper deserved the hazmat spill on their property for overloading him. He then resealed the bag with duct tape. The driver said he reweighed the truck and was legal. The driver said he had driven to my scale where I had stopped him.

I put the driver out of service for his actions. I considered jailing him but decided against it. I called his company and explained they had two hazardous material spills to clean up. One spill was in Arkansas at the point of shipment and one was here at my scale. I explained the company fine would be around $10,000 dollars. The company indicated they would be firing their driver.

I told the driver his fine would be around $5000 dollars. I explained he had spilled hazardous material from Arkansas to here and it would be impossible to clean it all up. Then I asked the driver, "do you have any other marketable skills beside driving a truck."

"Yes," he says, "I can run a backhoe."

I said, "This is great because you will probably never drive a truck again."

For years after this event I would have truckers coming from the same shipper (steel mill) as the driver in the story above. They would always ask if I was the one that got their friend whose truck was leaking hazmat. I would say, "yes, I'm the guy." Then without fail I would be told that he had a backhoe job in Arkansas. Seems I helped the hazmat driver find his calling... a backhoe!

CHAPTER 38
HEPING OUT THE POST OFFICE

My first year as a police officer (1987) had me being assigned to East St. Louis, Illinois. This town of 40,000 people had one of the highest rates of murder in the nation. Crime of all sorts was rampant. The reason first year officers get assigned here is due to the unattractiveness of the location. Once the new officer gets some time under his belt (seniority), he/she bids out to a more attractive assignment. A new hire then takes the place of the officer that bids out. Thus East St. Louis had a continual flow of officers beginning their career here and then leaving as soon as possible.

Back in 1987 nearly all the residents of East St. Louis received some form of governmental assistance. Jobs were scarce here. The governmental assistance came largely in the form of a check. On check days (early in a month) small crowds would gather around housing projects mailboxes to await the mailman. There was good reason to wait for your check. Often thieves would grab someone else's check and forge a signature. If your check were the one stolen, it might take another full month to get your much needed benefits in the form of a replacement check.

The old Sergeant called us in one day and explained that tough guys (thugs) were taking other people's checks at the mailbox sites. The sites might have a box with thirty individual boxes in it. This method of mail delivery meant as many as 30 checks might go to a single location. The Sergeant asked us to be on the lookout for these thugs and grab them if the opportunity arose.

I'm driving downtown East St. Louis and see a group of two tough looking guys sticking close to a mailbox. My old Sergeants words about grabbing some mailbox thieves are still ringing in my ears. So I stop and check out a guy by the mailbox. I spin him around and check for weapons and sure enough the guy is packing a pistol. I go to place him under arrest and he says "I'm an police officer for the U.S Postal system. I'm on a stakeout"

I stopped immediately. I had never been informed the U.S. Post Office had police. It seems like old Sarge should have provided this information as it would have been important on this assignment. I found the guys badge and felt foolish. I quickly released my fellow officer.

Well I did not catch a check thief that day. All I really accomplished was foiling a stakeout that had a good chance of working till I gave the postal police officer's identity away. I did gain valuable information... there are postal police and they were hard at work in East St. Louis.

CHAPTER 39
HELPING THE FEDS

The federal branch of law enforcement and corrections is huge. I seldom worked with the Feds. This story is one of the few times I did.

I was told to go to the Marion Federal Penitentiary and assist them on a prisoner escort. Now at that time Marion Penitentiary was the only level five institution in the world. In order to explain a level five institution let me explain how the Federal system worked. Normally, a prisoner would go anywhere but Marion. Then once in the system, if the prisoner begins to break rules or attack staff, they would end up transferred to Marion. With the normal situation explained, let me add the abnormal. If you were a mobster and had ties to those who could break you out of prison, you could possible begin your sentence here. That means only the toughest and meanest federal prisoners got there.

I arrived and security was beyond anything I had ever previously observed. Multiple corrections officials were involved. My job was to simply provide the lights and siren. I led an escort to an airport.

Once at the airport, I was relieved to be done. I spoke with a person involved in the escort. I asked why I was needed. I was told the prisoner escorted was a major mobster. I was told there was a worry the mob would shoot up the escort with a large gun.(I'm supposing a bazooka or something) I asked the guy what vehicle they would shoot at. With a smile he said, "why the first vehicle of the escort."

Glad I didn't know that till it was over!

CHAPTER 40
HUNTING THE RAILROAD KILLER

State troopers stop around six to eight vehicles per day. We find all sorts of people in the cars we stop. Good people and bad people drive the expressways of our nation. The trick is to pick out the bad people before something bad happens to you. Once and a while we do unusual things: like being involved in the hunt for a serial killer. This is my story of a hunt for the serial killer Angel Resendiz.

Resendiz rode railroad cars as a form of transportation to get around the country. He would jump on an empty freight car and ride till he had a fancy to disembark. When he disembarked, Resendiz killed people at random. If my memory is correct, he is credited with killing around 15 people. In 1998 Resendiz, killed a two people in the small community of Gorham, Illinois.

One of the small communities I patrol in and around was West Frankfort, Illinois. Shortly after the killings in Gorham, a young woman phoned the 911 emergency line of West Frankfort Illinois Police Department. The woman was hysterical and claimed she had been hanging out laundry and had been grabbed by a man. She said she thought the man had come from a nearby railroad car. She said she thought he was the railroad killer.

Every cop around responded to the report of the serial killer being spotted in West Frankfort. County deputies, West Frankfort City officers, and available State Troopers responded. My Sergeant came to West Frankfort with a plan. He wanted to walk the railroad from four miles North of West Frankfort back into the city. Once there he wanted to search each railroad car for Resendiz.

I was ordered to meet with the Sergeant four miles North of West Frankfort. We parked our cars and locked them up. I took my shotgun out and loaded it with buckshot. I figured if I had to shoot at Resendiz I wanted buckshot because you don't have to be nearly as accurate as with pistol ammo. Buckshot shoots about a 3 foot area at 30 yards so even if my gun sight is a little off I get my man.

It was hot summertime as we began our four mile walk. I was wearing a police vest. The vest made my body temperature higher than the outside air temperature which was in the 90 degree range. As I walked the four miles into West Frankfort, I was looking around every tree and berm for Resendiz. By the time I got into the rail yard at West Frankfort I was covered in sweat.

The number of rail cars in the West Frankfort yard was considerable. The railroad uses a set of sidetracks to park unused or unneeded rail cars. Naturally Sarge decided we must search them all.

Sarge was old and about to retire. He delegated me the task of checking each car while he observed. I would open the door to each car and warn that I was coming in and to surrender. When no response was given, I had to basically roll into the rail car. I could only see one half of the car upon entering. Once I was sure it was clear, I would look at the other end of the car. Needless to say if Resendiz were to be in a car with a gun on the side I could not see when entering I was dead.

Fifty railroad cars or so after starting this job I finished it. I was exhausted and dirty. I probably lost five pounds due to heavy perspiration.

Resendiz was not captured the day we had reports of him attacking the woman in West Frankfort. He later turned himself in and received the death penalty in Texas.

Capturing Resendiz would have been a great honor. Certainly an honor I would have liked to have received. Dying by his hand would have been a bad way to end a career. In the end, I'm glad I just got dirty, dusty and hot. I'm also glad this guy got arrested and could not harm any more innocent people.

CHAPTER 41
I WORK FOR U.S. TREASURY

The federal government has many policing agencies. All of us are familiar with the F.B.I. Less known agencies are Alcohol, Tobacco, and Firearms (ATF) and U.S. Secret service, just to name a few. This is a story about a traffic stop in which a man claimed to work with the U.S. Treasury Department. Treasury is responsible for enforcing laws regarding taxes and money.

It was 1991 and it was a hot 1 P.M. afternoon in the summertime. I was working I57 North of Benton Illinois. I observed a roll back tow truck (the towed vehicle is pulled by cables onto a flat deck behind the driver's compartment of the tow truck) with a red Isuzu four wheel drive SUV on its rear. The driver of the tow truck failed to signal as he changed lanes. I activated my emergency lights and got the driver to stop.

When I went forward to speak to the driver he had a wooden plaque in his driver's side front window. He immediately took it down. The driver handed the plaque to me. The wooden plaque had a set of alphabetical letters burned into it. Because the letters were burned into the wood, it took a second for me to put together what the letters said. The letters said "U.S. Treasury."

I asked the driver what he was trying to tell me. He said he worked for U.S. Treasury in the undercover division.

I look at this guy and he is certainly appears to be undercover. He has on an old oily t-shirt and equally oily jeans. He is sporting a long unkempt beard. I explain I could go to any flea market and get a burned wooden plaque that would read whatever I asked the designer to make it read. I tell him this plaque doesn't mean anything to me. I ask to see proper identification; like a badge. The driver says all he has is a plaque.

As I walk to my squad car, I step up on the rollback part of the tow truck and write down the 17 digit vehicle identification number (VIN) found on the Isuzu's dash. I run the VIN in the computer system to see if I have a stolen car. Bingo! The car is reported stolen from New York City. I run the driver of the tow truck and he has been arrested previously.

I go to the tow truck. I tell the driver he is under arrest for possession of a stolen car. I handcuff the driver and call a tow for the roll back unit and the Isuzu.

In my squad car the driver tells me this story. He claims this Isuzu was recovered by the U.S. military when they overran Panama the previous year. He said this car actually belonged to the Panamanian dictator Manuel Noriega, who was captured by the U.S. military. He said the car was given to the U.S. Treasury Department and made into a covert vehicle. Finally he swore to me he worked for Treasury and asked me to let him go.

At the time, I thought this was the craziest story I had ever been told. I looked at the young man and explained I was actually Santa Claus. I just appear to work for the State of Illinois.

The driver says I know my story is far-fetched but it is true.

I take the driver to jail and he asks for his one call. He dials a 20 digit phone number. He then hands me the phone. The man on the other end says he is a treasury agent from Washington D.C. and asks me to release this man. He claims the driver of the tow truck was in fact employed with the treasury department.

I tell the guy on the phone, "you can be anybody for all I know. How can I tell from a phone call who you are. No I'm not releasing your driver."

Shortly after the call I begin receiving faxes from the supposed agent. He sent faxes of his badge and Identification card. Then the faxes are followed by another call

The call comes from the supposed Treasury agent. I explain I am unmoved. Faxes don't prove the guy on the other end is an agent. The faxes only prove he has a badge, which could have been as homemade as the plaque I had originally encountered. The guy on the phone is upset and lets me know it.

So your upset I say. So what! I know the car is stolen. To get this guy released, you will take some kind of proof. Proof you haven't produced yet.

I end the phone call and work on my report. The phone rings again. Some guy claiming to be from the Illinois State Police directors office calls and asks me to release this driver and his tow truck. I give him a similar answer as I had the supposed treasury agent. I don't know who you are on a phone call: so no I will not release him.

Finally I receive a call from my direct boss. I clearly recognize his voice. He says he know the director of the Illinois State Police's voice. My boss says, "This is legit. The man works for treasury and release him and his vehicles." I press my boss saying, do you want the Isuzu released. You know it came back as stolen." I am told to release everything and "do it now."

I take the handcuffs off the driver. I take him to his truck. He is worried. Seems he only works for Treasury as a tow truck driver because he cut a deal to help prosecute an associate of his. The driver says he is way of route because he was going to see his girlfriend in Peoria. He is actually supposed to be in Ohio. Now he figures he may be fired and also prosecuted for his own treasury violations.

I thought I had put an end to this crazy issue but two days later I receive a call from New York City P.D. They want to know where the Isuzu is. They want me to take the stolen car out of the stolen car file. I explain my story and tell them to contact Treasury. I say I cannot remove the car from the file as I released it without returning it to its original owner.

Next I get a call from State Farm Insurance. They paid the victim of the lost Isuzu for his car long ago. Now they are entitled to the car. I tell them to contact Treasury.

In the end I figured this much out. The car belonged to some person in New York City. The car was stolen. The car ended up in Panama being driven by Manuel Noriega. U.S. Troops captured Noriega and took his car. The car was given to Treasury. Treasury failed to check the cars VIN against the list of stolen car VINS. The car was made into a covert treasury car. An x-offender was given the job of driving the car around on a tow truck. The offender was off route to visit his girlfriend. I was unlucky enough to stop it. State Farm learned they had not been given back a car they paid for. State Farm was contacting Treasury for the car or compensation. Me... I'm just a Podunk Police officer who figured this crazy set of events out!

CHAPTER 42
I-57 CHASE INTO WEST FRANKFORT, IL

I was gassing my squad car in West City when I was ordered on the radio to phone my post. This procedure was done when my command post did not want those listeners in scanner land to know a particular police issue. I phoned post.

I was told to proceed South on I 57. Marion P.D. had located a stolen car in Metropolis, Illinois and intended to follow it without attempting to stop it. I was to do the traffic stop. I was notified the driver was a parolee.

I drove South and when I saw the Marion cops following the stolen car all going Northbound, I still had to go South to find a turn around. Now I had to run hard (speed) to catch up. I caught the group near the Franklin/Williamson county line still headed Northbound. I was going fast to catch up and was in a marked car. I suppose the suspect saw the overhead lights on my car but in any case something spooked him and the chase was on.

We were hitting speeds of over 110 miles per hour. Oddly we passed the Franklin county sheriff. I recall he spoke my name over the radio and told me to catch the suspect. The suspect took the West Frankfort exit. I tried to get around him and shove him off the road so he would not enter the town but he nudged ahead of me. On Il Rt 149 in West Frankfort going Eastbound, I again tried to pass him but he forced me into oncoming traffic and I had to back off. We got to the railroad tracks and traffic was backed up. The suspect was forced to stop by traffic. I jumped out of my car and went to the suspect's vehicle. I attempted to break out his side window but failed. Traffic moved enough he was able to turn right and got away. I got back in my squad and drove East on IL Rt 149 while he paralleled me on a side street. I got behind him again on a street going South (Emma Street). He turned onto Cleveland street going West.

I'm still trying to stop this madman and attempt to pass again but almost hit some old lady who made no attempt to pull over. The suspect turns onto a dead end street (Short street) and now is going to have to go across an old removed railroad trestle. It has been raining and the suspect's vehicle gets stuck in the mud. The suspect flees on foot. My squad is also stuck: sunk to the rims in mud.

West Frankfort P.D. has been following the chase on radio. They are able to get ahead of where we were heading and capture the suspect. The suspect is brought to me handcuffed by Frankfort officers toting shotguns.

I get the information I need to make my case and turn the suspect over to Marion P.D. While awaiting tow trucks for the suspect's vehicle and my own, a fellow trooper comes up and explained a reporter had gotten so close that the trooper though he was a suspect. My fellow trooper had leveled a shotgun at the reporter. Hearing this I suggested he make up with the reporter with all possible speed.

Evidently the reporter was still unhappy. A complaint was lodged over this and the trooper evidently got some time off. I hated that my friend got in trouble but somehow it must have worked to my advantage. The state police had just initiated a new high speed pursuit policy. Since the stolen car did not meet the requirements for a pursuit, I was in violation. Due to the reporters complaint no one noticed my pursuit for three years.

Three years later I was called into the Captains office. I was informed I had the only pursuit in the district that was against policy. I excused myself and used a cell phone to call the Fraternal Order of Police (in effect my union representative). I explained my pursuit and asked if I was facing time off. I was told to go take a "chewing" as the brass had waited too long to make this a formal charge.

I went back to the Captain and got my "chewing". The last thing he said is I can't charge you with this as its been too long . I told my fellow trooper, who had pulled the gun on the reporter, about the Captain missing my illegal pursuit due to the reporter's complaint on him. We would often laugh that his time off saved me some time off.

CHAPTER 43
IS THAT ANIMAL BLOOD OR HUMAN BLOOD?

Imagine your worst nightmare! You meet this guy, he is big and strong beyond ordinary human strength. He is absolutely covered in blood. To make it worse, he has multiple guns in his vehicle. Certainly this scene has the makings of a Hollywood horror show. Well, I met this guy and here is the story.

The meeting was in the summer of 1988, in the afternoon, on Il Rt 34, three miles East of Harrisburg, Illinois. I saw an old box truck, with all kinds of rust holes in it, coming toward Harrisburg. The truck had an expired safety test sticker. In Illinois, in 1988, all trucks registered for over 12,000 pounds had to be safety tested every six months. The test was only $7.00 and if your vehicle passed the test, a sticker indicating the month and year of expiration was attached to the driver's side lower window. The sticker was large enough for law enforcement to read, even when meeting the vehicle on a two lane road.

I turned my squad car around as the truck passed me (it was going the opposite direction). I caught up to the truck and turned on my overhead lights. The driver of the unit stopped on the side of the road. As I walked up to the truck, a very large man stepped from the truck and he was covered in blood. Perhaps I should say dripping in blood.

I looked behind the driver's seat and there was multiple loaded weapons. I grabbed one which was a 30/30 carbine and jacked out its shells.

I was thinking on drawing down on this man but decided to cautiously check further. I asked, "is that animal blood or human?"

This huge man grunted, "animal."

I said, " if it is animal blood, where is the animal now?" (I was going to have to see this animal for proof)

The guy said the animal was a pig and it was in the rear of his box truck. He opens the box truck door and sure enough, a pig is hanging from the ceiling on a hook. This isn't a small pig; it appears to me to be a 300 pound pig.

I ask the guy how he gets the pig in the truck and he explains his whole operation.

The guy said he has a one of a kind business. He goes to the farmer's home. He shoots the pig. He puts the pig in his truck. He hauls the pig to his business and butchers it there.

The story explains what I have seen but I ask if the farmer helps him hang the dead pig. The guy says no he hangs it by himself. I ask if he uses pulleys or some device to assist him. He says no, I just lift it and put it on the hook by hand.

Now I have been a serious weight lifter for years but this is an incredible lift. A 300 pound wet bloody pig that gets picked up by hand walked into a box truck and lifted almost head high. So I feel sorry for my guy. I think surely he hasn't thought through a less taxing method of getting this pig in his truck.

I say why don't you lead the pig into the truck and then shoot it.

He says, "what and put a hole in my truck."

I look at the truck. It has rust holes all over in the box section. One more, or even a dozen more, bullet holes would make no difference. I feel like pointing this out, then I catch myself. I have just met one of the strongest men alive. His logic is lacking but his strength is admirable. So I let it go, no sense in trying to fix this one.

ADDENDUM

I spoke with the Sheriff of the county where this big guy resided. I told him how this guy was lifting 300 pound pigs and placing them on hooks almost over his head. The Sheriff said this guy was in fact one of the strongest men he had ever personally met. The Sheriff said he went to the guy's home to arrest him once for a domestic issue. The Sheriff said the guy acted like he was going to resist. The Sheriff told the guy that if he resisted he would be shot. The Sheriff said this man's strength was legendary in his hometown and anybody willing to tussle with him would be killed. Evidently the big man was afraid of bullets, as he decided to go peacefully with the Sheriff.

CHAPTER 44
LAWS

From far back into antiquity, man has made laws. Perhaps these older laws were more effective. The code of Hammurabi, which was in use in Babylon centuries before Christ, is a case in point. I understand this code was under 300 laws. With Hammurabi's code being under 300 laws, I am reasonably sure most of the people knew what was legal and what was not legal. Today in Illinois alone there are thousands of laws. I had a set of laws books for Illinois that comprised approximately 10 three inch volumes. There is no way for the common citizen to know most of these laws.

While most citizens don't know every law, we know enough of them to generally stay out of trouble. For example most of us know that possessing cannabis is illegal. What many of the citizens of Illinois did not know was that the legislature passed a cannabis tax stamp law in the 1990's. This law said to possess cannabis you must first contact the Secretary of State of Illinois and purchase this stamp for $100.00 to have the cannabis. No cannabis user would want to notify the government that they intended to possess an illegal substance so no stamps were ever sold. Later the Illinois Supreme court overruled this crazy law due to citizens being arrested on two counts (one for the cannabis possession and the other for not having the stamp) for a single act of possessing cannabis.

I do recall the time I was running radar on the interstate between Benton Illinois and West Frankfort, Illinois. I clocked a car at about 20 miles an hour faster than the posted speed limit. I got the car stopped and it had two young men in it. I asked the driver for his driver's license. The driver retrieved a shaving bag and was searching for his license in it. While he searched, I held my flashlight so he could see inside the kit. I could see the contents of the bag as well as the driver. When he finally handed me the driver's license, I told him to hand me his cannabis stash, as I had observed it. The driver complied and I placed him under arrest.

    I got the driver to jail. I told him he was under arrest for possession of cannabis. The driver was not in the least bothered, as he knew he had violated the law. Now I asked if he had his cannabis stamp for his cannabis. The driver asked, "what cannabis tax stamp." I kept a picture of the tax stamp with me so I could show the violators what the tax stamp looked like. The stamp looked like a postage stamp with a cannabis plant on its front side. The guy looked at me like I was from outer space. He asks how he could get a cannabis stamp. I explained the procedure already addressed above regarding the Illinois Secretary of State and the $100.00 costs.

    The violator comes unglued. He says what kind of idiot that uses cannabis would put in an application with his name and address in order to get a tax stamp.

    I explained to the violator I was sure he was correct. If the violator had turned in his cannabis tax stamp application saying he had cannabis in his possession then I am reasonably sure he would have been arrested before this incident tonight. Had the violator done a tax stamp application, a warrant would have been issued and a drug team would have searched his home prior to today.

    I left my violator shaking his head. Even this pothead was smarter that to buy a tax stamp and yet now that he was caught he needed a tax stamp. Nothing like good government!

CHAPTER 45
MIDGET THROWING

I must admit I lack any medical knowledge on midgets. I recall seeing the movie "Wizard of Oz" which contained a great number of them when Dorothy arrived in Oz. I also recall going to a town on the Alabama coast and seeing a sign on a bar announcing a midget throwing contest. I checked and evidently the bar had hired a midget to put on a football suit and then allowed contestants to toss the small guy into a set of mats on the floor. The longest toss won.

I don't think midget throwing is politically correct. I suppose if the midget isn't injured and makes a fair wage for his services then perhaps he is the real winner of the contest. My attempt at midget throwing was not intentional nor did I have any malice in my heart toward any midget.

The story begins on an afternoon in the summertime about 1987. I was driving my squad car in the passing lane and I observed a truck tractor trailer unit that I was passing had it's right turn signal on in order to turn into Marion, Illinois. The truck tractor right rear blinker was working but the blinker on the right rear of the trailer was not working.

I activated my overhead lights and got the unit to stop. I walked up to the truck tractor and spoke to the driver. I explained that the trailer rear turn signal was not working. The driver clearly had an attitude. The driver's voice was such that when he said "really" when I told him of his violation, he did not believe me.

I told the driver to meet me behind his truck and to leave the blinker on. I explained I wanted him to see his problem (i.e. no right trailer blinker) for himself.

The driver said "do I have to?"

I said yes; I do not want to issue you a warning ticket without your seeing for yourself the problem.

I went to the rear of the trailer and waited and waited. Finally I hear an agitated voice saying "okay I see the problem." I look down and the man was a midget. This surprised me as I did not recognize this when I was speaking to him and looking from ground level at him up in the truck.

We went to my car and I wrote the midget a warning citation. I told him he was free to go and he said "Oh no, you have to get me back in the truck." I asked how he normally got in the truck. The little man said his wife would put a ladder up beside the truck and he would climb in. I asked how he out of the truck in order to use the bathroom and was told he did not get out of the truck but carried a container so he did not have to get out.

With all my questions answered, I could see I would have to put him in his truck. We walked to the truck. I could see that boosting him up by the legs would not work as he was too short. I decided to take him by his large belt and by the back of his work shirt and toss him in.

I asked him what he thought of my idea and he said "whatever works." I opened his door took him by the belt and shirt and gave him a good toss. Unfortunately my aim was not good. The little man was far heavier than I had anticipated and I tossed him into the side of his truck. The poor little guy hit his head with a thud. I did manage to keep him from falling on the ground. My midget friend was dazed but I tried again and this time got him inside the cab of his truck.

I am thankful cell phones were not in serious use in 1987. I am reasonably sure someone would have reported seeing an officer tossing a midget into the side of a truck. As it was, my midget friend got off with a warning citation and a large bruise on his forehead.

CHAPTER 46
MY SEAMSTRESS

A seamstress is a good person to know if you are a Trooper. Uniform Pants come in long lengths and have to be shortened and sewed to have a professional look. Uniform shirts are manufactured wide for heavy officers. The shirts, in order to look professional, need taken in. The shirt must be tapered from the chest area to the stomach area and then resewn. I had such a seamstress. The lady was an older woman who was a friend of my mother. The lady's skills with needle and thread were unmatched. The seamstress made me look better than most of my officer friends.

One night around midnight, I was patrolling Orient Road. (Orient road is a small two lane blacktop running from Il Rt 149 into the small town of Orient, Illinois.) I would often patrol this road late on weekend nights. Orient had three operating bars and had what appeared to me to be heavy DUI traffic. I got behind a pickup truck that was going over and back across the center lane line. I activated my overhead lights and got the driver of the pickup to pull over. The driver, who was about 40 years old, was my seamstress' son.

The driver was worried. He was a professional truck driver and a DUI would probably end his career. Once he had performed the field sobriety test, I am sure his worries intensified as he was DUI. I placed him under arrest.

As a Trooper, I assigned anyone arrested with a first appearance date on their citation. I did this in the case of my seamstress' son. I would receive in the mail a subpoena to appear on the date assigned. The subpoena served as a reminder of the case for me.

I never missed a court date in 25 years of service but this one. I have no idea how I missed it. I received a written report that went in my file for missing this court date. It was not a fun ordeal.

My seamstress had been acting very cold during the period from the arrest of her son till I missed the court date. She was not interested in doing my sewing. Even though we were family friends, I could tell this relationship was over.

When I missed the court date, the DUI charge was dropped on the seamstress' son. I am reasonably sure he continued as a professional truck driver. I am also reasonably sure his mother was happy for her son's good fortune.

One night my wife and children were out of town. I came home with a pistol that I intended to unload. I always pointed my weapons at the bed and dropped the magazine out of the pistol onto the bed. Then I would remove the bullet from the chamber. I had done this procedure thousands of time without an accidental discharge. Well my luck ran out and just as I went to remove the bullet from the chamber….BAM…it goes off. The shell went through the bedspread, both sheets, and mattress cover into the mattress foam.

I thought "what is the wife going to say about this." It wasn't looking good for me. I was never going to hear the end of this mistake especially since I had assured the wife I would never have an accidental discharge. I had pointed out I was a professionally trained Trooper and checked and rechecked my weapons for bullets prior to putting the weapon away.

I grabbed all the items with holes in them. I went to see my seamstress. Surprisingly she was glad to see me. She took the gunshot items and repaired them to the point no holes could be located without knowing where the holes were prior to her work.

I put the bedding back on the bed and the wife was never the wiser.

I have thought about my seamstress since then. Even though I accidentally missed her sons case, I believe she thought I intentionally missed hers sons case for her benefit. I think she must have tried to repay me by doing an extra good job on my gunshot bedding. My seamstress is gone now... I sure do miss her sewing skills!

CHAPTER 47
OH, DEER!

Southern Illinois is a beautiful place. The area is well watered and is full of green vegetation. Some of the vegetation is consumed by whitetail deer. Our deer are some of the best in the country for size and strength. The deer proliferate well here so we have large herds.

On the night that this story occurred, I asked some of my fellow scale employees to come with me to dinner at a local truck stop. Two to the truck weigh inspectors (TWI's) decided to accompany me.

At the truck stop, we were enjoying a pleasant meal when my headquarters radioed me that a deer was up against the fence on the highway in front of the truck stop. I was told to keep it off the highway and prevent it from causing a car/deer crash.

I asked for the county animal control officer to be sent to my location as I would try to corral the deer. I went outside with my two friends (the TWI's) and we found the deer up against the fence just as I had been told. We formed a loose perimeter around the terrified animal and waited on the animal control officer to arrive.

The animal control guy arrived in his truck. He came over to us and announced "I don't do deer."

I'm like "what do you mean you don't do deer. You're the animal control guy."

Well, he explained I do possums, rats, raccoons, dogs, and cats but not deer. Deer are beyond the scope of my job.

I asked if he did not have a tranquilizer gun and I was told no. I look around and we are in a heavily traveled area with cars and shoppers. Killing the deer by bullet looks very problematic. I could not afford to let a stray bullet hit some passerby.

I asked the animal control officer if I can put the deer in his truck (if I can tie it up) and he agrees to let me. My plan was to have all my guys approach the deer simultaneously. I would jump the deer like a rodeo guy that does calf roping. I would wrestle the deer down and together we would tie it up. Finally we would load the deer in the truck for transport to the Crab Orchard Wildlife Refuge which is about five miles away. This plan might work as the deer weighed probably less than 100 pounds.

As we approached the deer simultaneously, the deer bolted. One of my assistants, instead of sticking his hands out to redirect the deer, runs away creating a gap in our line and the deer bolts out into the traffic lane. SMACK ! The deer is hit by a car. The very thing I was supposed to prevent just happened.

The deer goes flying and the car instead of stopping accelerates. Vroom, I hear the car drive off. The driver of the car who hit the deer must have had some issues. I suspect he/she was a suspended driver or lacked insurance. In any event, I was thrilled I did not have to answer to the driver why I had let the deer onto the road.

Now my radio is cracking and my headquarters wants to know if I (Car 13-88) have taken care of the deer problem. I smile as I pull my portable radio from my belt. I respond to the inquiry," affirmative 13-88 has taken care of the deer problem."

CHAPTER 48
OOOOOH, THIS IS BAD!

Sometimes other people are "in the know when you're not." It is like the practical joke that you're the victim of. Those involved know what is going on and you don't have a clue. So you look at others and nothing makes any sense. So it was with this case, till sometime later when I was given the information, that made it all make sense.

It started out easily enough. I was in Benton Illinois on East Main Street. I stopped a car with Georgia registration for lacking a headlight. I stopped the car directly in front of the jail. I walked forward and spoke to the driver and explained I needed his driver's license. I was handed a Georgia driver's license.

The driver's license check showed my driver was valid in Georgia but "Revoked" in Illinois. This man could legally drive in 49 states but could not legally drive in Illinois. The check showed my driver originally lived in Benton but had moved to Georgia. Before leaving Illinois the driver had gotten suspended on a DUI, then he got revoked for driving while suspended. Rather than correcting his driver's license problem, my driver had moved to Georgia and gotten a new license.

I said Billy Bob (not his real name) you need to get out of the car and he complied. I said Billy you need to turn around as I'm going to handcuff you as you have a revoked Illinois license.

Billy Bob turned around and said, "Ooooooh, this is bad!"

I said Billy Bob this isn't that serious. Why with a hundred dollars you will be out of jail before I get the paperwork done.

Billy Bob again said, "Ooooooh, this is bad!"

I had a deputy come from the jail and walk Billy Bob into the facility.

Several weeks later I got a court subpoena for Billy Bob for "felony driving while revoked." I showed it to my wife and told her I was baffled because in 20 years as a police officer I had never seen a Felony filed on a revoked driver. I explained to her without the word felony attached, the guy would normally do eight days in the county jail and get a fine. I told her the word felony meant a conviction would send Billy Bob to prison from 1 to 3 years.

I drove to the county courthouse on the day listed for trial. Normally a first appearance would not mean a real trial. As a rule the defense attorney asks for a delay or presents a motion that delays the real trial. So I was not expecting to testify and I was relaxed. Surprise, surprise, the trial went forward. I was called to testify first thing. Within minutes Billy Bob was convicted and given 1 to 3 years in the state prison.

I spoke to someone on Billy's situation. I was told Billy was stealing everything in Franklin County that was not nailed down and so far the police knew about it but had failed to catch him. But by George we had proof he was driving while felony revoked.

As I departed the courthouse, I saw a deputy was pushing Billy Bob's head down so he did not smack it on the car. Billy Bob was heading to Menard Penitentiary. I could also clearly hear him saying, "Ooooooh, this is bad!"

CHAPTER 49
OVERLY DESENSITIZED

This story starts when I was seven years old in 1963. I lived in Frankfort Heights, Illinois. The Heights was the area of town built on a tall hill. The town started in the heights and then moved West when the railroad came West of town. In the heights was a small market called the Heights Market. The store had a complete set of grocery items including meat. The customer would pick out his/her choice of meat by pointing through a glass refrigerated meat case. The clerk then took out the meat and operated a "band saw" to cut the meat into individual portions. The remainder of the meat was then put back into the meat case till purchased by the next customer. The store was operated by a small lady named Gerry.

My father would always take me to the Heights Market on Sunday. This was when most stores stayed closed on Sunday but the Heights Market would stay open seven days a week. The store had fresh doughnuts on Sunday mornings. One Sunday, I went with my father to the store at opening time and surprisingly it was locked. There weren't any lights on and there were no signs of life in the store. My father put me on his shoulders and had me look into the building. I could see the meat case in the back of the store but the case blocked my view of what I still believe to be a murder scene.

Gerry had somehow been forced to put her head on the band saw tray. Her head had been forced through the saw. She had been decapitated. If it had not been for the meat case, I would have seen her beheaded body. As it was, I told my dad I could not see anything wrong in the store.

A few hours later Gerry's decapitated body was found inside the store. There were two suspects and both of them were people my family knew well. Forensic science in 1963 was nonexistent and due to being unable to prove this case a murder, it was ruled a possible suicide. One of the original suspects lived into his 80's. The man never admitted his involvement but did say he was afraid to die and meet his maker. Evidently something bothered this suspect until his death.

My family was traumatized by the event. Gerry was a very close family friend. I played with her son. We would look at comic books together. Our family traded at Gerry's store exclusively. My mother counted Gerry as one of her closest friends. One suspect lived near us and the other just blocks away. I remember my family all slept in the same bed for a night or two after Gerry's death. Since I was only seven years old, the suspect who lived closest to me always made me nervous after the incident.

The Heights Market incident slowly faded away from my memory. In 1987, at 31 years of age, I was sent to the Illinois State Police academy in Springfield, Illinois for training. Part of the training was to view hundreds of photos of horrendous murders and accidents. The purpose to the training was to desensitize the new officers to death and human trauma. Slide after slide would show missing arms, legs, and other body parts.

I am doing my best to view these disgusting photos when a picture of Gerry's separated head is flashed upon the screen. A small statement is given to the new officers about the picture and then we were off to the next photo. While the other photos were difficult to observe, Gerry's photo bothered me. I will survive this but it still is visible in my memory bank to this day. I guess the desensitization worked as being around people who were dismembered never bothered me. I guess you could say I was overly desensitized.

CHAPTER 50
PEPPER SPRAY

Most police carry a number of weapons on their duty belts. Our duty belt weapons included a pistol, a collapsible baton, and pepper spray. The pepper spray was made of real chili pepper in concentrated form that was carried from the container by a liquid agent. If a suspect was sprayed in the eyes, he would not be able to open his eyes, much less see. His sinuses would drain creating heavy tears and a snotty running nose. He suspect would have trouble breathing and experience severe burning on his pores and in his eyes. The suspect would no longer be able to fight or resist. My best comparison to pepper spray use on a suspect is to compare it to Wasp spray which downs Wasps. The Wasp spray ends any fight in the insect and pepper spray does the same on humans.

One evening, when I was working at the I57 Northbound scale in Williamson county, the scale master from the Southbound scale across the highway phoned me. The scale master said he had a truck driver whose license was suspended at the Southbound scale. The scale master needed me to arrest the driver as he was limited to writing overweight citations.

I drove across the highway to the Southbound scale. I located the driver on the scale's parking lot. The driver was a big blond headed man. The driver appeared to be 6'3" tall and weighed near 300 pounds. I noticed he was wearing a confederate tattoo on his right shoulder.

I introduced myself to the driver and asked if he was aware his Commercial Driver's License from Georgia was suspended. The driver replied that he was unaware of his suspension.

I explained to the driver that I needed $100.00 in cash bond. The driver replied he did not have that much money.

I saw the driver had a female in his truck and asked if she was his girlfriend. The driver said she was his girlfriend but explained she did not have the $100.00 I was looking for.

I told the driver we needed to go into the scale house. He followed me and I explained he needed to call his trucking company and they could authorize a trucker's check. We kept the truckers check at the scale and the trucking company would phone a trucker's check company using a credit card and would be given an authorization number. The company would call us with the authorization number and we would verify it with the truckers check company. With the authorization number verified, the check would be the same as having cash bond.

As I explained this to the driver, he was becoming agitated. He looked at me and said, "I'm not calling my company."

I said if you don't give me $100.00 you go to jail.

He replied, "Where I live you don't give a hundred dollars without getting something in return."

I explained what he got for the hundred dollars was his freedom.

He said, "I'm not giving you one hundred dollars and I'm not going to jail."

Reasoning with this obstinate man was not working. I grabbed his arm and spun him around, with his face against a scale house wall. I got one hand handcuffed but each time I went to get the free hand this guy would pull away from me. I cracked his head on the wall and stepped back taking my pepper spray out. I sprayed him as he turned around. He ran across the room blindly and I continued to spray. He literally ran into the opposite scale house wall.

As my suspect ran and I tried to spray him, I had also sprayed the scale master. The scale master was also down in the floor from being sprayed. I got the scale master out and then the suspect. The spray inside the scale was overwhelming to even me. We were all outside the scale house now hacking and coughing. We had a water hose on the outside of the scale and I used it to spray water on my suspects face as he was the most affected person. My scale master was begging for water as well, so I would alternate between the two men with the water.

The scale master recovered fairly quickly that night. From that day forward when he even saw the possibility of my using pepper spray he would begin inching out of harm's way.

I took the driver to jail. I asked why he had resisted. He said where he came from in Georgia it was a matter of honor and a person was expected to resist an arrest.

The driver was now charged with driving while suspended and resisting arrest. His bond was now two hundred dollars. At jail he produced a credit card but it was good for only a hundred dollars. Ironically the credit card was sufficient to get him out till he resisted.

I drove back to the scale later and the drivers girlfriend was there. I explained to her that her boyfriend was in jail for fighting with me. She promptly threw all his clothes out of the truck and started her unit. She rolled off without her man.

The trucking company phoned me the following day asking me what had happened. I explained the driver was placed under arrest for being suspended and then began fighting me. The trucking company replied the driver was fired as of now.

Looking back this driver really screwed up. He lost his freedom, lost two hundred dollars, lost his girlfriend, and lost his job. All these things were lost for some kind of twisted Georgia honor of resisting when arrested. Go figure!

CHAPTER 51
POLITICS

I am glad to be an American. America offers more freedoms to the individual citizen than any country in the world. Part of the reason for our freedoms is our form of government; we are a republic. We, as citizens, vote for elected officials, who then represent us. The problem with this form of government is sometimes the elected officials blur the line of justice. That is to say the elected officials try to decide who the police arrest and who they don't. The elected officials usually act in behalf of one of their political supporters instead of letting justice take its course. When I hired on at the Illinois State Police, I thought that was behind me but I was wrong. This is the story.

I was driving on Il Rt 148 in Herrin, Illinois at around 1 A.M. I observed an old pickup truck turn onto Rt. 148 ahead of me. The driver was over the lane divider lines and I activated my emergency lights and got the truck to pull into the parking lane of the road. The driver was a perfect gentleman but was very intoxicated.

When I arrived at the Williamson County jail, one of the female tele communicators said to me, "ooh you got a bad one."

I thought the tele communicator was telling me this man was a fighter with the police. I responded to her remark that this man had been nothing but a gentleman.

The tele communicator then said, "you will see what I mean."

I got the drunken driver to the breath machine and he was pleasant. The driver provided the necessary breath and was jailed.

As I sit down to write my report, the female tele communicator yelled to me that I had a phone call. I picked up the phone and it was the Sheriff elect (he was not yet Sheriff but had been elected). The Sheriff elect asked if my arrested driver had given breath.

I replied the driver had blown into the breathalyzer.

The Sheriff elect said something like, "well I guess I'm too late" and hung up the phone on me.

I was bewildered by all the actions of the Williamson County people on this man and no one would further enlighten me.

A few days later I went to attend a funeral with my Master Sergeant. A Sheriff from another county had lost a son in a car accident and we attended the funeral visitation. After leaving the funeral home, I went to get into my car and radioed in as required. To my amazement I was ordered to patrol the distant Jefferson County instead of my normal patrol of the southern half of Franklin County and all of Williamson County.

My Master Sergeant heard the order and picked up the radio microphone and told headquarters this was his shift to run and I would be going to my normal patrol. Radio responded the Captain had personally given the order for me to head north to Jefferson County.

Now Jefferson County is a great county but being sent there meant I would not be able to eat at home. Eating at home was my only time to see my children during weekdays. I worked night shift, so I could not see them at night. I did not see them in the mornings when they were in school. Needless to say I was upset about my new patrol. I pressed the Master Sergeant but he had no idea what had happened. Not knowing what else to do I demanded to meet the Captain.

I got to see the Captain. Now the Captain up till this meeting had always liked me. I had been in the top ten officers in prosecuting DUI's in the state for three years. I had actually had the second highest number of DUI arrest in the state for one of those years. Those stats made the Captain look good and in return he had treated me well. I expected this meeting would go well but it did not.

The Captain explained he had been contacted by a State Senator who had been contacted by the mayor of Herrin. The Captain said I had arrested the president of a Civic organization. (I won't name the organization but it was one where people help others in need but tend to drink a lot at their organizational buildings). He said perhaps I should stay out of Herrin. He thought drunks were not as dangerous in a town.

I lost it. I said perhaps you should explain drunks being less dangerous in town to Mothers against Drunk Drivers. I said it's funny that I was a great officer for years bringing in those DUI arrest awards to the district but now you have a problem with it. I explained the Captains job was to rein me in if I was making bad arrest but not to punish me for a valid arrest. I said, "Great! I will be on the interstate if you want me in the future."

I left the room. Evidently the captain was thinking of all the awards the district was going to lose because he called me back into his office. The Captain told me the Senator who contacted him had a lot of clout. The Senator voted on our budget each year and we shouldn't offend him.

I was not impressed. One Senator seldom passes or holds up a budget. I explained the political realities to the Captain. I also explained his order was keeping me form seeing my children the one hour a day I normally had available.

The Captain said I could come back to my normal patrol if I stayed out of Herrin. I said fine I will be on the interstate. I said if I Can't be in Herrin, I won't be in West Frankfort, Benton, Marion, or any other small Southern Illinois town. I left the room again only to be called back into the Captains office a third time.

The Captain tried to deal with me. He understood there are quantitatively more DUI's in towns than out of towns and he was messing up a good thing he had going. Finally he said if I stayed off the streets with taverns, particularly 14th and 16th Streets in Herrin, I could go back to my normal patrol.

Sensing this was a last best offer, I accepted it.

Several weeks later I was in Christopher Illinois. I had pulled over a car for a seat belt and was issuing a citation. Low and behold, up came the Senator in person.

The Senator informed me I should be patrolling the interstate not towns.

I asked the Senator what my arm patch read… State Trooper of Highway patrol?

The Senator responded State Trooper but wanted to know what that fact had to do with where I patrolled.

I informed my State Senator that Troopers could in fact patrol anywhere in the state but highway patrol was limited to the highway. Wisconsin has a Highway patrol, which only patrols the highway. Illinois has the State Police which patrols the state. I explained to the Senator this difference was in fact set forth by the legislature which he was a part of.

When the Senator huffed off after my lecture I phone post and spoke to my Master Sergeant. I explained I had been harassed enough. I was going to leak this nonsense to the press.

"Oh my please no," the Master Sergeant replied. Evidently my bosses feared the press far more than one Senator. What do you want us to do the Master Sergeant asked?

Anything to get this guy off our backs I replied.

The Master Sergeant met with the Captain. That weekend an Illinois State Police roadblock was held in the Senators home town. (This had never been done before due to the small size of the community) The message that was to be sent is keep politics out of our police work.

I never heard from the Senator again either directly or through the Captain!

CHAPTER 52
PRAYING

I am a Christian. That is to say I believe in the resurrection of Jesus Christ. As a believer, I often pray to him and expect that he gives results to a prayer of faith. Working for a government entity can make the decision to pray a risky decision. This is my story on my prayer and its results.

I was on the interstate 57 about 9 P.M. on a cold winter night. I was checking the speed of motorist between Benton, Illinois and West Frankfort, Illinois. I looked up and a northbound vehicle was traveling at a high rate of speed. I locked the radar on and the car registered 89 miles per hour in what was a 65 miles per hour zone.

I activated my overhead lights and pulled the car over to the emergency stop lane. I went forward and spoke to a female who was probably in her mid-thirties. I explained the reason for the stop (her speeding). I asked her if there was a valid reason for her speeding.

The woman said she did not have a reason.

I walked back to my squad car and wrote her out a citation. I returned to her car and gave her the citation and explained what she needed to do with it. My job was now finished and I prepared to leave when she said, "I really don't think I was going 89 miles per hour."

I explained I had locked her speed on to my radar screen and would be glad to show her the speed reading. I told her I did not want her to go away thinking I had manufactured her speed. I wanted her to know I was truthful.

I let her get out of her vehicle and thought she was following me. I opened my squad car door so she could see the radar reading and then realized she had gone to the passenger side of my car. So I stepped into my car and popped her door lock so she could open the passenger door and read the radar screen. I pulled the radar to her side so she could read it and to my surprise she sat down in my car.

The young woman reads the screen and says that I have obviously caught her at 89 miles per hour. She now proceeds to cry. I think the tears are over the citation and begin to work with her on how to get court supervision to keep her driving record clear and get a time payment plan on the citation if she lacks the funds to pay the citation.

The young lady says she is crying because she has just come from the doctor who said she has a failing heart, which will require a heart transplant. Trying to help, I suggest she get a second opinion. The woman replies this is the second opinion. She said the news she just got had taken her mind off her driving which is why she was going so fast this evening.

As much as I would like to help this woman I cannot. First I don't know for sure she is truthful. I have had more stories on why people speed than Carter has liver pills. Some are true and some are not. I usually don't except stories on speeding unless I can verify them. I certainly could not verify her heart condition. Secondly and more importantly, once a citation is issued my agency did not allow me to cancel it. The citations were numbered and I am accountable for each number. If a citation goes missing I have to give a reason for why it is not turned in. So I explained to this woman to take the citation to the States Attorney's office and they can dismiss it if they choose to.

I have said all I can say at this point but the woman still sits in my car crying. I explain I am a Christian and if she would allow me to, I would turn in her first name (without her last name) for prayer at my local church. The woman says, "That would be wonderful" and "I would really appreciate your prayers."

The woman is still in my car and is still crying deeply. I ask if she wants me to pray here and now and she says, "Yes would you."

Without touching the lady, I pray that the Lord might repair her heart. I finish praying and the lady is smiling. She thanks me for my prayer and concern. She leaves my car and continues to her destination.

Several days pass. One evening I hear the district on the car radio having officers call post to speak to the Master Sergeant on duty. My car number is 13-88 which is among the largest number in the district. I am the last one told to call the district.

I phone in and the Master Sergeant is curt. He says have you prayed for anyone on the interstate lately.

I reply that is a vague question, anyone could be praying on the interstate.

The Master Sergeant replies have you prayed for a woman with a heart condition on the interstate between West Frankfort and Benton, Illinois.

The old Master Sergeant was a wise guy. He knew all along it was me who prayed but he went to all the trouble to have all the other troops deny praying. He knew of my Christian values and that I prayed regularly. He also knew he had me with the full story of the ladies heart condition.

"Yes it was me," I replied to the Master Sergeant but how did you know.

The Sergeant said another Troop was given the job of reading local newspapers for stories on Trooper activities. A local reporter had written a story on my praying for this poor woman and yet still giving her a citation. He said the story portrayed our agency in a negative light. The Master Sergeant said I would be given a written reprimand for praying.

I tried to explain the reporter got his story backward. The citation was written before I had knowledge of her heart condition. The Master Sergeant was unmoved and wrote me a reprimand. The reprimand stayed in my file for three years and any further praying would result in a more serious level of discipline.

I phoned my lodge which acts as a labor union. I asked if I could beat this reprimand. I was told I could in fact win this issue but the department would look for a reason to fire me if I did. I decided to live with the reprimand.

A year or two later my daughter makes very close friends with the reporter's daughter (the reporter who wrote the negative article on my praying for the lady with the heart condition). This reporter's daughter is involved in a serious car crash. My daughter contacts me and wishes me to go with her to the hospital to pray for her friend. I agree to go to the hospital for prayer.

At the hospital, the reporter's daughter lies between life and death. The reporter is in the waiting room as I arrive. He knows and I know, about his article that caused me so much grief. I ask the reporter point blank, "do you want me to pray for your daughter."

The reporter says, "Yes, will you please pray for her."

My daughter and I proceeded to pray for the injured young woman.

Years have passed since that day the reporter's daughter lay in the hospital. I have heard from good sources the reporter has become a believer in Christ like me. The reporter's daughter has recovered and has married and had a child since that day. So was the prayer on the interstate worth the reprimand... "Absolutely yes."

CHAPTER 53
SAVING THE GIRLFRIEND FROM DROWNING

One afternoon I was on patrol near Benton, Illinois. It was a hot summer day in August, with temperatures around 100 degrees. Here in Southern Illinois, it was Du Quoin State Fair time. Heavy traffic was going both directions on Illinois Rt 14 that runs from Benton to Duquoin. Fair attendees were filling the roadway.

I received a radio alert from my Du Quoin Illinois State Police headquarters that a man was trying to drown a woman at Il Rt 14 and Rend City Road. This location was about two miles West of where I was so I floored my cruiser and headed to the location I had been given. As I drove I was asking myself "where there was enough water to drown anyone at the location I was given."

When I got to the location of the attempted drowning, I could see multiple cars blocking the roadway. I parked my squad car behind the traffic and began running on foot some hundred yards to where I could see a gathering of people. There in the middle of the crowd a guy was trying to drown his girlfriend in a mud puddle formed by a chuck hole in the road that had collected water from the previous night's rain.

The little woman, who appeared to be less than 100 pounds, could barely push her head up and get a breath then her boyfriend would shove her under the water again. I knocked the suspect off the woman then began wrestling him in order to handcuff him. All of a sudden a mammoth brown arm reaches over and pushes the suspect down and locks him to the ground. It seems our largest Trooper who is at least 6'6" tall and 300 pounds had arrived. (I sure was glad to see him).

After getting the suspect under control, I spoke with the victim. The victim said she and the suspect lived together. Today they had decided to go to the fair. On the return trip a verbal fight had ensued. The suspect stopped his car right in the middle of the road and dragged her out. He took her to the mud hole and was attempting to drown her. Not one of the 30 to 50 people who were there did anything to assist her. She said if I had not arrived when I did she would have died.

I had seen crowds of people act this way before. It seems when there is a crowd of people it is more unlikely for someone to step forward and act in support of a victim than when there is only one or two people present. If there is a crowd, a situation develops that I call "diffuse responsibility" takes over. No one is responsible to help because it's someone else's problem. In this case a crowd of 30 to 50 people almost let a woman be drowned without doing something to assist her. I felt like yelling at the crowd, "Wake up people and protect the weak among you!"

CHAPTER 54
SHIRLEY'S HOBAR AND THE GOATS ON THE ROAD

Tele-communicators are very important people. They are considered the lifeline to the police. They track all the patrol officer's activities and advise them of incoming calls for assistance. If an officer fails to call in within five minutes of a traffic stop, they begin to call out his/her car number. If no response is received within two minutes of the car's number being called, the tele-communicators send out assisting officers. We officers consider the tele communicators invaluable.

For whatever reason, most of the tele-communicators are female. The tele-communicators with years of experience very seldom get rattled, no matter what the emergency. Their voices stay clear and calm. They continue to be unfazed in anything from a murder to a police officer down call. The newer tele-communicators get rattled. The officer hears it in their voice and often times things don't go smoothly in communications with them. This story is about a newly hired young female tele-communicator who got rattled in her first month on the job.

There was a notorious bar in Williamson County, which at the time of this incident was called Hurley's Show Bar. The bar was just outside the city limits of Johnston City Illinois. Being outside Johnston City, meant calls for assistance from the bar were routed to the Williamson County Sheriff's office.

A call came in for assistance at Hurley's Show Bar as a fight was in progress. The young female tele- communicator took the call. In her haste to get officers to the scene she put out a broadcast to all cars, "there is a 10/10 (fight) at Shirleys Hobar and all available cars should report there at once."

Every officer listening knew a 10/10 (fight) at a bar is serious business. We usually react by turning on our lights and siren and proceeding to the scene as fast as possible to prevent a death or serious injury. The problem was no one knew where to go.

There was silence on the radio. Usually responding officers would be saying 10/4 Car 13-88 is in route. 10/4 car 13-4 is in route, etc. But the radio sat silent as the officers tried to figure out where Shirley's Hobar was. Finally a bright young deputy figured out the riddle. He asked if tele-communicator did not mean Hurley's Show Bar. Yes she said that was where we should go to.

Immediately the radio began to bark with officers heading to Hurley's Show Bar. The result of the incident was the young lady being stuck with the nick name Shirley.

Shirley stayed on in spite of her nick name. She later was involved in giving me some bogus information.

I stopped a car and the driver informed me there were some goats on the roadway a few miles back. I informed my tele-communicator of the goat on the highway issue. I believe Shirley was listening to my radio traffic as she called to me that she thought this was a new federal program for feeding goats. She explained the goats were being allowed to graze in the median area between the lanes of the interstate.

I intended to overlook Shirley as I knew full well the Federal government was not going to be grazing goats in the median area of the interstate. The number of car/goat wrecks would be high, not to mention car/other crashes where the drivers were avoiding the goats.

Unfortunately my Captain overheard the radio traffic from Shirley. He went ballistic that anyone would think the government would approve of goat grazing on the interstate. He made his feelings on the matter known on the radio and I'm sure hurt Shirley's feelings. I never heard Shirley transmitting on my frequency again. Too bad, she was a nice young woman!

CHAPTER 55
SOCIAL SECURITY

Social Security is a good idea. The working man pays in and then when he/she gets old the system pays the worker back in monthly installments. The intent in establishing Social Security was to provide for the aged in their elderly years when holding a job would be difficult or impossible. Later after Social Security was established for the oldest Americans, others who were disabled or sick were added as those who would receive benefits. While the second group is problematic due to the length of years they receive benefits, the worst group to collect benefits are those who get them by fraud. This story is about a man who collected Social Security for seven years by fraud.

Many years ago I received a call from a young mother in her twenties who wanted to report her father as fraudulently receiving Social Security. The lady said her father had gone to an optometrist and received a slip saying he was legally blind. She said her father submitted the slip to Social Security and received benefits of $18,000 per year for seven years. She said her father went to the same optometrist and got a slip saying he was within visual limits to drive a vehicle. She said her father submitted the second slip to the Illinois Secretary of State and received a Commercial Driver's License. She said her father now drives a truck/tractor trailer unit which is in her mother's name. The lady said her mother's name is on the truck so it appears she (the mother) drives the truck and receives the income from the truck. The lady said her mother did not drive the truck and actually worked full time at a local retail store.

While this was an interesting story, I was shocked the lady would turn in both her father and mother in the scam. I then asked "why she wished to tell on her mother and father."

The lady explained her father had raped her repeatedly as a child. She said her mother was aware of the situation and did nothing to stop the abuse. She felt a little justice would serve them right.

I checked out the situation and the lady had described the situation accurately. The father was driving truck and receiving Social Security. The truck was in her mother's name and the only work the mother did was in a retail store. I got all my documents together and interviewed the parents. I was done with the case except for needing proof from Social Security that payments had been given to the father.

I phoned Social Security. I finally got to the fraud section and explained my case. I was told I could not receive the requested information. I was told the father would be dropped from the payroll.

I protested vigorously. I said what would happen to a person who went to the bank and demanded $126,000 in a robbery and received it.

Why they would go to jail the fraud investigator said.

Correct I replied. Yet this guy just robbed the U.S. government of 126,000 and you are just going to take him off the payroll.

That's what we do said he investigator and hung up the phone.

Well whoever says crime doesn't pay has never duped the Social Security System back in the 1980's. I sadly reported to the lady who had started the case that her father had been taken off the Social Security payroll. I explained that nothing was going to happen criminally. This lady had been victimized by her father and now the government.

CHAPTER 56
STEPPENWOLF

Some people want to live as others. Usually these people want to live like a famous person. I have seen Abraham Lincoln reenactors who go beyond the requirements of the job. They attempt to take on the whole persona of Lincoln. In my little town, we have a guy that when he puts on a cape and certain clothes becomes Elvis Pressley. No I don't mean he thinks he looks like Elvis, he thinks he is Elvis. Thoughts like these are certainly a little over the top, huh? Well this is a story of a guy that thought he was Steppenwolf.

If you are a young reader, you may well wonder, who is Steppenwolf? In the 1960's there was a band called Steppenwolf. There lead singer had a very raspy type of voice. The voice was so different as to make it clearly discernible among artist of the era. The truck driver I came to deal with did have a voice that matched the lead singer of the band Steppenwolf.

I was working at a scale in Madison County Illinois. The Illinois State Police was in the middle of a truck blitz. I would finish one inspection and immediately have to go to the next. They called this week Road Check, it was a nationwide set of truck inspection put on by the United States Department of Transportation (USDOT). Each state in the Union was to do their part in inspecting trucks.

In comes this bright red truck. In addition to the required truck name and USDOT numbers, this unit had the word Steppenwolf across the top and on each side. The writing was in cursive and very distinctive. I stopped the unit for an inspection.

When I walked up to the driver, the reason for his nickname being Steppenwolf was obvious, it was his voice. I looked inside the cab of the unit and it was like no other truck I had ever seen before. The bunk area of the truck was filled with mirrors. The bunk bed was covered with a shag blanket. The bunk was also blessed with multiple speakers that went to a stereo sound system. Steppenwolf described his bunk as his love den.

Steppenwolf dressed the part as well. He wore a fancy shirt and jeans. He was certainly dressed beyond my average trucker. Steppenwolf also appeared to indulge in body building. Steppenwolf muscles stood out among truckers.

I realize all "lovers," like this man Steppenwolf, don't use drugs to ply their ladies affections but this guy might well be up to that angle. He had invested a fortune into his love den, why wouldn't he add a little cannabis to the mix? This was my thinking as I asked Steppenwolf if he had any drugs in the truck.

Steppenwolf was adamant there were no drugs in his truck.

I checked old Steppenwolf's Criminal history. Bingo! A felony conviction on drug possession plus a prison sentence for the same.

I told Steppenwolf of my suspicions and of his previous drug incarceration. I told him I wanted to search his truck for drugs.

Steppenwolf says, "I dare you, in fact I double dare you to search my truck. You won't find any drugs."

I told the Sergeant of Steppenwolf's dare and that I was going to search the truck. The Sergeant watched Steppenwolf as I did the search.

I stepped out of the truck and told Steppenwolf that I had good news and bad news for him. The good news was that there were no drugs in his truck. The bad news is that I had just found a pistol in his shaving kit. I said, "Steppenwolf, as a convicted felon, you cannot possess a firearm."

I placed Steppenwolf under arrest for possession of a firearm by a felon. I towed his truck and notified his company of their cargo's location.

The company did not know Steppenwolf was a felon. Steppenwolf had lied on his application. The company fired Steppenwolf. So Steppenwolf ended up in jail on a new felony and lost his job.

If there is a lesson here for Steppenwolf, it's "blend in." Steppenwolf's attempt to be a super lover had caught this cop's attention and led to his downfall.

CHAPTER 57
"TANK" TROUBLE

As a former coal miner and resident of Southern Illinois, I have seen many nicknames. Some are the exact opposite of the person's characteristics. For example, anyone with a nickname of Tiny is probably very large. If your nickname is Colgate, you lack teeth rather than having a full set of teeth. On the other hand sometimes a nickname fairly accurately portraits a person. I recall a guy knowing who went by the name Quaterloin, who was as big as a side of beef. Two fellows, known as Box of Rocks and Ox, were men who were really mentally slow. One name that reoccurred in the coal mines was "Snake". Anyone with the name of Snake was to be watched as they tended to be underhanded. This story is about a man nicknamed Tank because he was huge. Tank was also different in that he had lost a leg from the knee down in a motorcycle accident before I came to meet him.

On the night I met Tank I was on Herrin Road just East of I57 in Williamson county. At that time there was a nightclub called "Hurleys" there. I observed a red van headed East from Hurley's and it was literally all over the road. I activated my overhead lights and got the vehicle to stop. The driver was "Tank" and he was biting the passenger's back as I got to the van. The passenger, a smaller male, was screaming. I grabbed Tank and he quit biting the passenger.

I got the keys from the van and went to check on the passenger. The passenger had shed his shirt and was screaming that Tank was an animal. The passenger had bite marks on his back but was not bleeding. I asked if he wished to press charges and he said no. The passenger said he just wanted to leave. I got the passengers personal data and let him walk away.

I got Tank out of the van and had him lean on the side of the vehicle. Tank was without his prosthesis (wooden leg) and could not stand long. I checked Tanks eyes for horizontal gaze nystagmus (a condition that people who are intoxicated have in which their eyes involuntarily twitch) and his eyes showed he was intoxicated. I placed the big man under arrest and handcuffed him in front.

I nearly always handcuffed suspect's hands behind their backs so I would have less of a chance of their becoming combative but I needed Tanks help. I was going to try to help Tank hop to my squad car. Since he was huge and drunk this meant letting him have his hands out front would assist his balance as we tried to get to my squad car.(Tank was probably 6'1" and weighed 275 and was all muscle. Tanks arms were huge from using crutches for years.)

Tank assisted me in getting him to my car. I got him in the front passenger seat and went to attach the seat belt. As I reached for the seat belt, the big man lifted me to the ceiling of my squad car. My legs were dangling. I told Tank to put me down. He laughed and said what are you going to do about it. I said "Tank if you don't let me down I'm going to hurt you." Tank wouldn't let me down. I thought of poking his eye but decided to grab his finger. I snapped his finger back and he screamed in pain and let me down.

I called for a cage car from county (not all squad cars came with cages in those days and I you needed one you had to ask for one). Some county deputies came and got Tank. We hopped him to the cage car and took him to the jail.

The following morning was my day off. Unfortunately I had failed to check the vehicle identification number on the van Tank had been driving. I had to go to Herrin Illinois and see the van. I decided to get my children some doughnuts and then drive to Herrin.

As I drove to the doughnut shop, I saw Tank on crutches standing beside the highway hitchhiking. I stopped my private car to speak with him. I explained I was going to Herrin to see his car and would give him a ride. Tank said he would rather rot in hell than go with me. I told Tank no one in their right mind would give him a ride and I would be back in an hour and he would have changed his mind by then.

An hour later I arrived and sure enough there was Tank still attempting to get a ride. Tank was tired of hitchhiking and decided he would ride with me.

I am a Christian and as I drove Tank to get his van I got to tell him of the eternal life he could have in Jesus. Tank was trapped as he needed my ride. He was not too happy with my company or my witnessing to him.

I had not seen Tank for years and I was at the courthouse to testify on another case. I was standing in the lobby when a large hand popped me on the back. I was hit hard enough to have to catch my balance. When I turned around there was Tank with a big smile on his face. Tank introduced me to his pastor and exclaimed he had become a Christian. Tank told his pastor that I had witnessed to him.

I asked Tank why he was at the courthouse if he had become a Christian. Tank said it was from old arrest prior to his accepting Christ. I was glad to hear it.

Several years went by and I decided to open an old murder investigation. A young man had been killed in Williamson county while parked on a bar parking lot. There was very little to work on but Tank had been at the bar with his biker buddies when it occurred. I discovered Tank was in Oklahoma. I go his number and called him. The prime suspect was a very feared biker and I knew Tank, being in Oklahoma, might be willing to tell me what really transpired 10 years earlier.

Tank said he did not see the murder but gave me a possible witness' name. Tank said he was still walking with Jesus.

About a year later I heard of Tanks death. I know where he is today but am unsure of how he died other than it was natural causes. Perhaps the years of drug and alcohol abuse had its toll. In summary, Tank was my brother and friend.

CHAPTER 58
THAT CAR IS ON FIRE MISTER

As a State Cop I have fought many, many car fires. Sometimes the fires have been so intense that I start stopping Semi truck tractors in order to get extra fire extinguishers. I have seen a few people burn to death. This is a more humorous fire Incident.

I was driving down IL Rt 159 in Swansea, Illinois. I saw a brown car that had an engine fire. The driver had gotten a blanket and was attempting to smother the fire out. That is to say he was wrapping the fire with the blanket to remove the oxygen from the fire.

Removing oxygen from a fire will work. Using a flammable item such as this blanket probably will not work as the blanket itself is combustible and would light and burn.

I pulled my squad in front of the burning car so I could get to my fire extinguisher and more quickly (it was kept in the trunk) and put the fire out. I got my fire extinguisher and went to work. The fire was out in seconds and I breathed a sigh of relief. The damage to the engine was negligible and this car would run again.

I had the car's driver come to my squad car and begin writing him a report so his insurance company would have record of this fire. The report would insure my driver got paid for his damage.

All of a sudden a young man from the gas station across the road was knocking on my window. The young man was very excited and said, "That car is on fire mister."

I was parked in front of the car I had just extinguished the blaze in the engine. So while I could not see the car, I was sure the fire was out. I told the young man that what he was seeing was smoke from an engine fire that I had already extinguished. The kid said "it's blazing sir". I looked in my rear view mirror and the car was blazing but this time from its trunk.

This was a four alarm car fire. I had to call the fire truck to put this car fire out. It seems the driver, after I had put his engine fire out, had put his blanket into his trunk. The blanket was on fire and the driver did not realize it.

So after the fire truck left, we (the driver and I) sat there. The car was now totaled. The engine had received some damaged but the trunk fire gutted the trunk and backseat area of the car. So I wrote a second report describing the trunk fire.

The two fires were separate events and had to be reported on separate reports. I always wondered what the insurance company representative thought of two fires in the same day on the same car; one in the engine and the other in the trunk.

CHAPTER 59
THE CAR JACKERS CHASE IN JEFFERSON COUNTY

Carjacking is a very personal crime. The perpetrator at gunpoint demands the automobile of another. So in addition to the loss of the vehicle, the victim has been face to face with a pistol. The victim will forever be traumatized.

In the case that follows, the suspect car jacked a car in Michigan and began a ride to a southern destination. The suspect, aged around 25, picked up his younger brother (who was 16 years old) to have as a riding companion.

North of Mt. Vernon, Illinois the two brothers were running short on gas. They stopped at a gas station and filled up their small green Pontiac. Lacking the money to pay for the gas, anyone reading the story would have expected a drive off would have occurred. Here the gas station would have lost the normal cash for a sale. However, the older brother of the duo now decides to perform an armed robbery. At gun point he has the clerk empty the cash into a paper bag and the duo sped away.

Running from any crime is difficult for suspects. Cars just don't outrun electronic radios. The gas station attendant phoned 911 and reported the armed robbery. Another dumb mistake made by this duo was the decision to flee on the interstate. With limited exits and entrances, the probability of being captured increases.

A car from district 12, which is North of Mt. Vernon observed the green Pontiac and began to pursue the suspects. The pursuit was Southbound on I57. The suspects were not going to stop despite being followed by a squad car with lights and siren activated.

I was riding in the passenger seat with another policeman. We saw the case coming. We got behind the suspect. At the I64 intersection the green Pontiac shot across the interstate and headed Westbound in an Eastbound lane. We were running at speeds of aver 120 miles per hour. The driver of the Pontiac was playing chicken with oncoming traffic. I thought he was using the oncoming traffic to try to cause them to crash into our car. I pulled out my pistol and rolled down the passenger window. The policeman driving the car I was riding in sped forward around the Pontiac but I did not feel justified in taking the shot. I did make sure the driver saw me pointing the pistol at him.

At the Woodlawn exit, the suspect driver went the wrong way on the exit ramp and got off the interstate. The chase continued up Woodlawn road. The driver was still playing chicken with oncoming traffic trying to cause a police crash behind him. The driver eventually ended up in Mt Vernon Illinois. Since this chase was being radioed as it occurred, Mt Vernon P.D. had cars awaiting the suspects arrival.

In Mt. Vernon the two suspects fled their car on foot. Both suspects took refuge in a drained swimming pool. They were captured at gunpoint without any shots being fired.

Since I did not make the actual arrest (Mt Vernon P.D. did), my partner and I drove to Mt. Vernon P.D. to do the paperwork and interview the suspects. The younger brother of the two was not involved in the carjacking and apparently did not know his brother was going to do an armed robbery of the gas station. So we called his mother and she began the trip to get her son.

The older brother was in tears about being captured. He did not try to hide his crimes as they were very apparent (we had the car and the gun). He looks at me and asks how long I think he will spend in prison. I did the math on his armed robbery and carjacking. I recall telling him I thought 18 years before good time was taken into account would seem close. He breaks into sobs and tells me that he is really a "good person." The suspect says this is so unfair.

I got the suspects attention. I explained he was not a "good person." I told him good people don't stick guns in other people's faces and take cars and money. I informed him his schooling had given him a case of "invented self-esteem."

When I left him behind bars, I really don't think he got it. I think he had no idea of the pain he had caused others. I suppose with at least nine years in prison maybe he figured this out.

CHAPTER 60
THE COLLINSVILLE CHASE

In 1987 I was patrolling I-64 between E. St. Louis and Fairview Heights Illinois. I observed an older vehicle with expired license plates going Eastbound on I-64 and pulled the car over. The driver gave me his license and I ran a computer driver's license check on him. The check showed the driver had a warrant from Madison County for a library fine that was unpaid. (Note: in 26 years as a cop this was the first and only library warrant I encountered). Madison County said they would extradite the driver. So I placed him under arrest.

In arresting the driver, I had him face away from me and searched him prior to handcuffing him. In the search I found a badly burned spoon in his pocket.

For readers who are unfamiliar with drug use, most drugs come in powder form at sale. The drugs are then mixed with water and put in a container like a spoon and then heated with a BIC lighter. The heated mixture is held in the spoon to cool then a syringe is used to suck the drug mixture up. The drug user then ties off his arm (could be leg but arms are used more often) till the user's veins rise. The syringe is then used to inject the mixture into the user's vein.

I checked the spoon and the residue on it was heroin. I informed the arrestee that he was under arrest for possession of heroin. As I drove the arrestee to St. Clair county jail, he began to appeal to me to get him recognizant bond. He explained he was broke and would not be able to make cash bond. He also said since he was white

(Caucasian) he would be unable to eat in jail as his food would be forcibly taken from him.

I asked him what he could give me as an informant to make it worth my while to assist him. The arrestee said he could turn me on to a stolen car if I could find a way to get him recognizant bond.

In any county but St. Clair, the county provides deputies to take the accused to the courthouse to make their first appearance before a judge. In St. Clair County, I had to show up the following morning to check the prisoner out of jail and take him before a judge.

The first appearance is required for all felony arrest. At the first appearance the judge will advise the arrestee of the charge against him/her. The judge will ascertain if the defendant has an attorney or can afford one. If an attorney is beyond the arrested persons resources, the judge will appoint a public defender. Finally the judge will set cash bail for the accused.

When the judge announced the bail required as $50,000 with 10% to apply (in plain words this defendant needed $5,000 in cash to be released from jail), I spoke to the judge. I explained the defendant was offering to lead me to a stolen car if he could get recognizant bond (here only a signature would set the defendant free). The judge agreed that if the defendant's information led to an arrest and a recovery of a stolen car recognizant bond would be issued.

I took the defendant back to jail and went with him to an interrogation room. The defendant told me this story. He said a 20 year old male named Robby Rattiner (this is a made up name) was living with a older female Doxie Doolittle (also a fabricated name) in Collinsville Illinois. Doxie was employed in St. Louis Missouri and had a very good job. Doxie had a brand new black Monte Carlo SS which she allowed Robby to drive. Robby had totaled Doxie's car while high on drugs. Robby had grown up with a father that did car body work. Robby knew how to do a VIN (Vehicle Identification Number) switch. So Robbie stole an exact match car to the one he had totaled. In plain words he stole a brand new black Monte Carlo SS. He took the Vehicle Identification number found on a metal tag in each car's windshield and replaced the stolen cars VIN with the wrecked cars VIN.

So Doxie's car she was driving looked exactly like her original car. If anyone looked at her cars VIN it was a match to her original car. Doxie was happy as she had a new and undamaged car again. Unfortunately someone lost their brand new car from auto theft for her to be happy , but that was fine with her and Robby.

My source gave me the exact location where Doxie and Robby lived in Collinsville, Illinois. I drove to that location and observed a new black Monte Carlo SS in the driveway. I went to the Madison county States Attorney's office and filled out the paperwork for a search warrant on the car. I was refused a search warrant because my confidential informant had not been used before and therefore under case law could not be trusted as a source (if he proved trustworthy on this case I could use him in the future).

I had observed the Monte Carlo in the drive and saw it had very tinted windows and could be stopped on the road for violating traffic law. I contacted my Sergeant and he agreed to assist me by providing me with two backup cars. I intended to stop Robby and Doxie as he brought her home from her job in St. Louis Missouri. I planned the stop on the belt line road in Collinsville.

I checked with Collinsville P.D. and was told they had dealt with Robby before. I was told he always fights with officers and is thought to be carrying a small nickel plated automatic pistol. Robby was threatening to shoot the next cop who tried to stop or detain him.

We set up on the beltline. I was the middle car. Sarge had wanted the oldest officer among us to make the stop. This guy was also an expert on confidential VIN's. (these are vehicle identification numbers on the engine, frame and other locations). It was snowing and was dusk as the first car saw Robbie pass. The oldest officer turned on his overhead lights and gave pursuit. Unfortunately Robby wasn't stopping. I got a radio message from the 1st car that he was couldn't keep up with Robby in the snow. I began to give chase and radioed the third car to assist. The officer in the third car said his car wouldn't start. I chased Robby down a dead end street. Robby turned his car sideways in the snow and exited. I saw a flash in his hand and thought it was the nickel plated automatic pistol.

I drew my Smith and Wesson 38 caliber revolver (remember this is 1987) and screamed at Robby to stop. I could see the chamber on my revolver turning. Robby stopped and fell to his knees with his hands in the air. I let the trigger back down easily so as to not discharge the gun. I handcuffed Robby and realized what I had seen in his hand was not a gun but was his car keys. (looking back 30 years I am thankful I was packing a revolver as an automatic pistol would have discharged killing Robby).

The car was stolen. I took Robby in to Collinsville P.D. for interrogation. A couple of Collinsville officers asked how I got Robby to surrender. I said I guessed I just spoke his language. In fact what had happened is Robby had seen his life flash before his eyes. He had cried all the way to jail that he believed I was going to kill him when I drew down on him. He was right in that it was a very close call.

CHAPTER 61
THE DOG WHO COULD NOT SMELL

The Illinois State Police had several canines during my time as a State Police Officer. I would not have wanted to be a canine officer. The dogs shed, smell, and bark almost nonstop. The officer's day is crammed with dog feedings, brushings, training, and an occasional veterinarian visit. In addition, I have seen some dogs run off and others bite their canine officer.

The major advantages of having a canine is having extra help in an emergency and locating drugs. The extra help can be lifesaving. Most officers have a button on their side that when pushed lowers the rear window on their squad car and lets the dog loose. The dogs are trained to come to the officer's aid and bite those resisting arrest. The sense of smell of the canine is very useful in finding narcotics. The dog can often locate hidden drugs on smell alone. I have seen two types of hits by canines for drugs. Some dogs are trained to sit upon the locating of drugs and others are trained to scratch. The sitting dog to me is preferable since the suspect remains unalarmed to the dog's signal.

With all this being said about canines, my 70 year old mother came to me in around 1995 and asked me to assist her and others in procuring a dog for my hometown. If I recall correctly the dog was to cost around $2,000. My mother proposed to provide $500 for her part of the dog purchase. I felt ambivalent about my mother's request. Like I have shown above dogs are both good and bad. Also the state police had dogs, so was a local dog really necessary. In any event, I kept my money and did not donate.

I had a car/deer crash occur about a half mile East of West Frankfort on Il Rt 149. When I arrived I opened the car up and was going to inventory the contents of the vehicle so the towing company or others would be less likely to steal the owner's belongings. As I opened the driver's side front door, I looked in the door side pocket and there was a good 50 grams of cannabis.

I had no sooner pulled the cannabis from the car than the local police officer arrived with the canine my mother and other good citizens of the community had purchased. The officer asked me to put the cannabis back into the car and let his dog locate it.

I was not too keen on this idea because as I have pointed out dogs are unpredictable. I did not want this dog to bust the plastic the cannabis was in and spill the contents into the wind. The local cop really wanted to test his new dog and begged me to let the dog try.

I relented and put the cannabis back into the door. The local officer took his dog round and round the car but got no response. The local officer then opened the door which had the drugs in it but got no response from the canine. Finally he pulled the dog to the drugs and held his nose upon the sack but still got no response. He pulled his dog back from the car and finally the dog sat down. The local guy was ecstatic and announced his dog had in fact alerted to drugs. Quite frankly I thought the old pooch just got tired of the entire hubbub and sat down.

This dog did not last long with the local department. I was not surprised because as the old saying goes "you cannot teach and old dog new tricks" and this dog either could not smell or would not alert on drugs.

My poor mother was very upset. She had provided $500 toward an unproductive canine. I told her she had done a good deed and not to let it bother her. I explained there were other better canines that could assist her beloved city's police department.

CHAPTER 62
THE DRUNK WAS CURED

When most people go to the hospital their cure is a slow process. My guess is the average hospital stay in at least three days. This is the story of a miraculous cure that took place in minutes after a hospital admission.

I was driving East on Il Rt 149 from West Frankfort to Zeigler, Illinois. I was behind a pickup truck that was having trouble staying in it's lane. This occurred in the 1990's before prevalent cell phones so typically that meant I was following a DUI. Before I could activate my overhead lights to pull the truck over, the driver pulled into a driveway beside the road.

I went forward to speak to the driver. I asked if he in fact lived here and found out he did not. I asked if he knew the owner of the house and he did not. The driver had spotted my overhead lights and tried to make it look as if this were his home.

A quick series of sobriety test and I discovered what I suspected. This driver was DUI. I handcuffed the driver, towed his car, and drove him to the Franklin county jail.

At the jail, when I helped the suspect from the car he collapsed. I thought this was an act similar to pulling into an unknown person's driveway but I was forced to go along with the ruse. I radioed my headquarters and asked for an ambulance to come and take my suspect to the hospital.

I followed the ambulance to the hospital. The suspect was still playing passed out. I radioed my headquarters and got a notice to appear due to the suspect being at a hospital and being unable to make bond which was $300.00.

The suspect was now acting awake and asked what a notice to appear was. I explained that the notice to appear was given so no bond would be required. My suspect asked what would happen to him. I said he was the hospitals problem now as I was leaving. My suspect asked "what if I just leave". I again replied that was between him and the hospital. "Would you chase me", he asked. I said "No".

At this point the suspect ran down the hall and disappeared out the hospital doors. I was surprised that being told he was not going to go to jail would cure a man so quickly.

CHAPTER 63
THE GANGSTER WHO SPIT

I grew up in the small town of West Frankfort, Illinois. This was a working class town of 10,000 people. The majority of those employed were coal miners. This was a town that had only white people. When I first arrived at my first post as a police officer in E. St. Louis Illinois, I had experienced very little contact with African-Americans or gangs.

E. St. Louis was probably 95 percent African- American when I arrived in 1987. While I stuck out as a white officer in predominantly black city, I can really say I had little problem with my race. The people of E. St. Louis treated me as well as my black counterparts. My black counterparts were sometimes called Uncle Toms for doing their jobs. The people seldom said anything to me about my race whatsoever.

The gang situation was somewhat different. The Gangster Disciples were making inroads in the high school but the gang I am speaking of was more akin to the Cosa Nostra. These were older men with a group of hired employees that forced others to pay protection money or help them get part of a government contract for construction projects.

One such gangster was a man I will call Sid. Sid's business was to provide trucks for excavation projects in E. St. Louis. When a government project was bid, Sid always managed to get a subcontractor status on the job. Rumor had it if Sid did not get to provide some trucks for every job bad things happened. They (bad things) happened directly to those who contracted the job or bad things happened at the job site that greatly increased the cost of the contractors doing business. Needless to say Sid had a booming business.

Sid understood that not registering his trucks at a cost of $2,000.00 per truck would increase his profit. I understood that it was my job to get Sid to pay the good state of Illinois what he owed them for registration.

I had three fellow black officers I worked with in E. St Louis. The three were all very afraid of Sid. The Sergeant came to me and asked that I deal with Sid. I agreed and called Sid into the St Louis Office.

Sid only had one eye. Supposedly someone had shot up his bedroom in the middle of the night and shot him in the eye and he lost it. Sid was also missing some of his front teeth and so he would spit when he got angry.

I got Sid good and angry when I informed him I would be checking on all his trucks for registration and would be issuing citations and doing an investigation if irregularities were found. Sid could see I was going to be getting into his pocket and came unglued. He ranted and raved about me picking on him due to his race. The spit was just a flying.

I told Sid I did not live in E. St Louis and I was not afraid of his reputation. I said this was a warning to get his trucks registered.

I would stop Sid's trucks shortly after our meeting. Sure enough several were not registered. I would issue citations to the drivers of the unregistered trucks. The citations cost Sid money and so did the down time on the trucks. Sid would come over to my squad car as I wrote his drivers the citations and call me names and basically have what my mother called a "hissy fit." I would barely roll my window down, just enough to hear Sid because the spit would fly. By the time I would drive off, my entire drivers side passenger window would be covered in spit

After a couple of days of my stopping his trucks, Sid got the message. Sid went out and registered all his trucks. I often wonder if Sid really couldn't help the spitting or just enjoyed giving a cop a good spit bath for dealing with him.

CHAPTER 64
THE LITTLE PIGS

Americans are a highly competitive people. We compete in sports, business, and life in general. When considering if Americans compete in life in general remember the saying, "are you keeping up with the Jones'." Police are no different. We compete in weight lifting, running, and team sports like Softball. Sometimes we compete at our jobs; for example in who can catch the most speeding cars. None of the competition requires the officer make up evidence; it just means the cop patrols more hours or is more diligent in locating a speeding car. Well this story is about such a competition.

I was in E. St. Louis Illinois in 1987 and was working for the Illinois Secretary of State Police. The Illinois Secretary of State Police take great pride in knowing a set of laws called the Illinois Vehicle Code (I.V.C.). Whereas the Illinois State Police receive two weeks of training on the I.V.C., the Secretary of State Police receives eight full weeks. The first two weeks of training for the Secretary of State Officer occur in the Illinois State Police Academy. Once graduated from the Illinois State police Academy, a recruit then receives an additional six weeks of training at the IVC School conducted by the Secretary of State Police.

When I arrived in E. St. Louis, I was challenged by the older officers to find the most unusual violation I could find. Then that violation would be compared with what the other officers found for the week to see who the group thought won. One of the earlier winners was an officer that found a truck with fewer seat belts than passengers. At first I thought this was a big deal until I learned all pickup trucks from the era I worked came with three seat belts. So if you see a pickup with four people in the front then one person is not going to be seat belted. Once I figured out the other officers system for finding vehicles lacking seat belts, I was unimpressed.

My own claim to fame came one day as I was driving down I64 in rural St. Clair County. I was passing a yellow school bus. As I went by the bus, to my great surprise, I could see all the windows on the bus had been removed. Over each window space was a metal bar which had been welded to the bus. My mind is racing. Is this a load of kidnapped kids? Rather is it a load of young felons somehow going to school on a bus?

Fortunately I could see behind the bars and what I saw was a load of pigs. The pigs seemed to be enjoying the ride and were sticking their noses out between the bars and the window opening. The driver had welded an enclosure for himself in the front of the bus to prevent the pigs from affecting his driving. The violation here was that the bus was still school bus yellow and had a stop arm still attached.

I activated my emergency lights and the bus pulled to the roadways edge. I went forward and spoke to the bus driver. The driver owned a hog farm. He said he got a very low price on the bus and bought it. The driver said he saved thousands of dollars on the bus when compared to the cost of a truck for hauling his hogs to market.

While I agreed with the driver he got a good deal on his bus for his pigs, I could not understand how he could stand the smell when driving it. The driver laughed and said he was used to it since he farmed hogs anyway.

I explained to the driver that when he purchased the bus he was required to change the bus's color to something other than yellow. Otherwise traffic around the bus thinks the bus is hauling school children. Further I explained the bus's stop arm sign must be removed. I said the arm is only to stop traffic from both directions when school children are embarking or leaving the bus. I wrote the driver a warning for his violation.

I took my warning to the next meeting the officers had in E. St. Louis. No one had ever seen a violation of school bus colors before so I won the competition. Everyone was so impressed that the contest was abandoned. I suppose you could say I won for all times sake.

As for the farmer with the pigs on the bus, he painted the bus green and continued to haul the pigs for some period of time. Quite frankly, I would have paid the difference and got a truck!

CHAPTER 65
THE MASTER SERGEANT'S GIRLFRIEND'S SON

Before I was a Illinois State Trooper, I was a Secretary of State (SOS) Investigator and an Illinois Commerce Commission (ICC) Police Officer. Both of these organizations are separate entities and do not answer to the Illinois State Police. The Police officers of the ICC and SOS would use the same radio system as Troopers but would rarely come into contact with them. Thus we would often upset Troopers by arresting their family members. It appeared to me some of the Troopers of yesteryear expected special treatment and while their fellow troopers knew who was to get the special treatment, the ICC and SOS officers did not. This is a story of my arresting a Master Sergeant of the Illinois State Police girlfriend's son.

I was employed by the ICC police in about 1980 and was in Eldorado, Illinois. Eldorado is a small town (maybe 4,000 people) and has two major two lane highways (U.S. Rt.45 and IL Rt 142) that pass-through town. The highways actually cross each other and have a four way stop light to regulate the traffic. I had pulled up to the U.S. Highway Rt 45 stop light at Rt 142 when a hot white 1979 Pontiac Trans Am pulled to the light beside me. The Trans Am was in the left turn lane and was to my left. A young man, who turned out to be 18 years old looked directly at me and began to rev up his engine. The light changed to green and the young lad began squealing his rear tires and turned his car sideways by squealing his tires to make the turn. I could not believe my eyes as I was in a marked squad car with lights on top and I was dressed in a police uniform.

I activated my lights and got the Trans Am driver to stop. The kid could not believe I had stopped him. He informed me his mother lived with a local Illinois State Police Master Sergeant. He further said his mom's boyfriend had said I was a truck police officer and could not arrest him.

The young man was kind of correct. The ICC police's function was to check trucks and no to bother cars. I was also on shaky ground in making this arrest because the powers to arrest that had been granted to ICC officers was pretty vague. Even so I was not the type to let this act go as his spinning the Trans Am around had come fairly close to causing an accident with a car that was stopped waiting for the light to turn green. I took the kid with me to a local business. I phoned Springfield and spoke to the ICC Chief. I explained what had just happened and that I intended to arrest this young man for reckless driving. My boss did not like the idea but said he would support me.

Reckless driving is a serious offense. The penalty can be 364 days in the county jail and a $10,000 fine. Nevertheless, reckless driving is just what I charged the young man with.

A local Eldorado cop came up and found out what I had done. He was ecstatic. He indicated the young man had been driving recklessly for a couple of years and his mother's boyfriend had kept him out of trouble.

I met with the assistant state's attorney. She said I had written an excellent report and justice would be served. According to sources the justice was a little light. The Master Sergeant had taken the young man's car away (evidently it was in the Master Sergeant's name). The young man was allowed to join the Army. All my charges were dropped.

Well at least the streets of Eldorado were a little safer for the driving public!

CHAPTER 66
THE MEETING

    During my 25 plus years of active service as a policeman, I had several Captains. Some were congenial, others were stand offish, and some were difficult people. One Captain stood out above the rest in that he was approachable if you worked hard but much less so if he considered you a time waster. This Captain was unlike the ones who proceeded him in that he was very muscular and wasn't afraid of a good physical fight. Rumor had it he was one of the best ground fighters in the world. He taught at other agencies on how to fall on your back and still win a fight, so I believe the rumor was true though I am unsure who rated him as being so good at ground fighting. So with this Captain the officer had the worst of all worlds. He/she had a Captain who would not only write you up for discipline, but who would physically intimidate you at the same time.

    We had computers in our cars in the early 2000's and would time to time hear the computer "bing" as it's bell announced that we had received a message. Sometimes the message would be from the Captain. It would often be in capital letters to almost scream at you. The Message would read something like:

    SOME OF YOU OUT THERE ARE NOT DOING YOUR JOBS!

    YOU KNOW WHO YOU ARE!

    IF THIS CONTINUES YOU CAN BE SURE WE WILL HAVE A MEETING IN MY OFFICE!

    After the message came out you could hear the hum of radio traffic increase as the Troops went to work. No Trooper wanted to be the one to have the meeting with this Captain.

Evidently the Captain had heard rumors of some complaining going on behind his back because he called a meeting of all the Troopers in the district. This was no small task as he had to get a neighboring district to cover patrol for us and he had to switch as many Troopers as possible to day shift. The date was set and we all arrived. The big Captain swaggered out in the middle of his people and announced, "I've heard there is a lot of complaining going on behind my back. I don't like this. Be man or woman enough to tell me to my face what your problems are."

You could have heard a pin drop. No one had anything to say for about two minutes so we just stood there. Finally a brave Trooper said I just want to point out the problems with the IWIN program. Now the IWIN program was a computer software program that allowed the Troopers to write a report and incorporate other documents and pictures into it. The problem was it was very difficult to operate. When it did work it in the writing phase, the report was often lost when we attempted to send it wirelessly to our supervisor. The Troopers hated the program; so much so that many Troopers had actually quit arresting people so as to not have to write a report.

At this point in the meeting several Troopers let go with similar gripes about IWIN. The big Captain took out his notebook and took a note as each man expressed his dismay of the IWIN system. I kept silent and watched in fascination.

The big Captain was getting the names of the complainers. Once all those who wanted to complain had said their piece he announced, "It is what it is" and walked off.

The Troops sat there stunned. Their complaining went nowhere. The IWIN system was not going to be fixed. The Captain simply got the names of those who would now have to start doing more IWIN reports.

CHAPTER 67
THE OSCAR MEYER WEINER MOBILE

Vehicles come in all shapes and sizes. There are big trucks, ambulances, small cars, buses, and things that I cannot describe that run on our nation's highways. When a police officer decides a law has been broken, he/she then must notify the dispatcher of the location of the traffic stop, a description of the vehicle, and the license number if available.

The acronym officers are taught for traffic stop is LOVELI. All incoming officers are taught LOVELI and practice it over and over. Lo is for location. VE is for vehicle. LI is for license. The call in must be in proper order. The dispatcher's computer screen for logging the traffic stop is actually ordered in the LOVELI sequence to increase the dispatchers speed in typing it in.

As an example, officer 13-88 calls in a traffic stop. He/she would say traffic stop on I57 (interstate 57) milepost 65, with a blue Toyota, Missouri passenger plate A145.

The rub is in describing the vehicle. Some officers get good at picking out the brands of vehicles stopped. Other officers simply say a "brown passenger car." If the vehicle is something other than a car it gets described. An example is a "green farm tractor."

Well Oscar Meyer did own a fairly large truck like vehicle. The vehicle looked like a hot dog in a bun. I suppose it was called a Weiner Mobile. The driver employed to drive this vehicle had a lead foot. Inevitably I would be on a traffic stop and this vehicle would pass on the other side of interstate. The Weiner Mobile would go fast enough I would see big numbers flash across my radar screen. I was not locking in the numbers as I was busy with my stop. I would try to do the right thing by notifying officers further down the interstate that the Weiner Mobile was headed their way at a very fast speed.

For example, when the Weiner Mobile would go by I knew several officers would be working at a truck weigh scale located in the direction of the vehicles travel. So I grabbed my cell phone and alerted the officers by telephone to stop it. Unfortunately Weiner Mobile was never located or stopped for speeding.

It finally donned on me what was happening. Nobody wanted to be the one to have to describe the Weiner Mobile on the radio for all the other Troopers to hear. The driver of this truck must have known this fact. He/she had the perfect vehicle to speed with.

I thought through the situation. I would stop the Weiner Mobile using the language of an " Oscar Mayer brown truck." Unfortunately I never got the chance to stop this truck. While I suppose I had seen this vehicle ten times before I hatched my plan for the stop, after this I never saw it again. I suppose it was for the best. The Oscar Meyer driver never got his speeding citation and I never got the name Oscar Meyer cop or worse!

CHAPTER 68
THE "POOPER"

As long as man has hated his fellow humans, disrespect has existed. Numerous times as a Trooper, I would be called to an incident between dueling drivers. The name they call this is road rage" and it nearly always started with disrespect; usually in the form of a one fingered salute. Spitting is another form of sever disrespect. I have seen spit fly when one person hates another. Perhaps the worst form of disrespect I can think of involves poop. This is a story of a young lady who had this form of disrespect down to a science.

Very late one evening (12 midnight), I was patrolling Orient Road in Franklin County. This little road was notorious for drunken drivers. I observed an old Buick going toward Orient Illinois and got behind it. The driver of the Buick was all over the road and I turned on my overhead lights. Instead of stopping the driver of the Buick, turned into the Denning cemetery.

Denning cemetery sits adjacent to Orient road. Part of the cemetery is fully visible from the road. The other part is not visible from the road. If a person goes over the hill in the Denning cemetery, it's like entering the twilight zone, as no one would know you were there. Naturally the drunk driver takes me over the hill. The car stops at a grave that had a rotating red light. Several (four) people jump out of the Buick and appear to be worshiping the grave.

I seldom called for backup but this situation had the markings of craziness and I asked for a backup. I got out and spoke to the driver. He was obviously drunk. The driver was from Louisiana and said he was visiting his cousin's grave. I took him through some sobriety test and he failed

I had not had any problems yet but had not called off my backup either. I knew I was going to handcuff the drunken driver and that is when problems usually start. I was handcuffing the driver when one of the females of the group attacked me. I will call her name "Mae".

I knocked Mae off of me and got the driver handcuffed even though he was also resisting. I tossed him to the ground and got Mae handcuffed also.

Now Mae was known among the Franklin county police as the "pooper". Actually she was known as the shi**** but I prefer the former name. Mae had been arrested by a County Deputy and while handcuffed behind her back, had pulled her own pants down and pooped in his car. The smell was always with the Deputy no matter how many times he had cleaned his car.

Mae was sentenced by a Franklin County judge once and decided to get even. Mae got on the Franklin county courthouse elevator and pooped in it too. The Judge heard of Mae's pooping in the in the elevator and tried to have her arrested. Police could not confirm she did it without DNA and the cost was prohibitive. She was never convicted.

My help finally arrived. A deputy and my own Master Sergeant arrived. My master Sergeant said he would take the guy and I could get the girl.

I protested the Master Sergeants decision. I said I needed to speak with the guy and I would take him and the Master Sergeant could take the girl. Quite frankly, I did not want the "pooper" pooping in my car. I also knew this Master Sergeant was fanatical on his car's cleanliness and thought it would be hilarious if Mae visited him with a big one. The Master Sergeant agreed he would transport the girl.

I got my guy to the jail without more problems. Several hours later, I found the Master Sergeant relaxing in the front of the Sheriff's office. I asked if he knew who he had transported. He said he did not. I explained he had transported the notorious "pooper". I received a cussing as he literally ran out to his squad car. I would like to end this story by saying the pooper left him a big one but that would be a lie. The Sergeants car was clean and all I got was a big laugh out of his frantic search of his car.

CHAPTER 69
THE RIOT

Southern Illinois is a conglomeration of small towns. Usually riots are expected in cities like Chicago, New York, or Los Angeles; not places like Herrin, Galatia, or Marion Illinois. Yet each of the Southern Illinois cities just named, all with fewer than 20,000 people, has had riots. Our Southern Illinois riots have always been union/non-union riots. The Herrin Illinois riot, between union and non-union men, in 1922 resulted in 21 people being killed. In 1981, a riot in Galatia Illinois left a non-union coal mine site burned. This is my story about the Marion power plant riot of 2002.

On the day of the riot, I was at the Marion Illinois scale. We, several Troopers including me, got a phone call to go to an area east of the Marion Power plant. The call came with the dreaded phrase "it's a riot and shots have been fired."

I followed another trooper with my squad and a third trooper followed me. As we were driving to the riot scene, I observed two parking lots full of cars and trucks at a business called King Tuts. The King Tuts was a gas station, motel, and unattached bar. I knew that King Tuts would never have that many vehicles in the parking lot. I immediately thought of my days as a union coal miner during the 1981 riot at Galatia, Illinois. The men that went to that riot had told me that they had met at a state rest stop and had crowed themselves into fewer vehicles. Those rioters said they left the majority of the cars at the rest stop so as to not create their own traffic jam at the Galatia mine. This information would serve me well later.

We arrived at the riot scene. Debris was everywhere. Multiple truck windows were smashed. Some of the non-union workers were still on the scene. Those non-union workers had various bruises and scrapes due to being in fights with the union supporters. One man said a union supporter was shot in the leg. A county deputy was on scene and had gotten things under control. The deputy was trying to get started on the paperwork on damages and injuries.

I told my two trooper buddies to follow me back to King Tuts as that is where the men involved had gone to. As we drove to the parking area of King Tuts, I was ordered by radio to return to the riot scene. I phoned in on my cell phone and spoke to my acting Lieutenant. I explained that the county Deputy had the scene under control and the only hope I had of catching those involved was to continue to the King Tuts parking lot. The Lieutenant agreed to let me see what I could find.

I got to the parking lot and it was empty except for three empty cars and one car full of people. The car that was full of people was pulling in to let the occupants out. As the people raced from the full vehicle to the three empty ones, my fellow officers and I pulled up to the group. I jumped out and said, "stop I need identification from each of you."

There were seven men who had just pulled up. Approximately three of the men wore t-shirts with a union logo on them. One man was bleeding from behind his ear. Naturally the men wanted to know why they were stopped. I explained that a non-union worksite had just been the scene of a riot. I explained windows had been busted and men injured. I explained I felt like I was on strong legal ground to make this stop. Years ago the Supreme Court had ruled in Terry versus Ohio that officers can make a stop (not an arrest) if they can articulate a crime has been committed or about to be committed.

Shortly after arriving, rain began to fall and I put the seven men into the three squad cars on the scene. My superiors arrived shortly and took control. No arrest was made on the scene but I produced a report.

That evening I arrived home and turned on the T.V. To my surprise several local politicians were on camera explaining that this riot was caused when the non-union men had attacked peaceful union protesters. I told the wife that obviously my case was not going to be successfully prosecuted.

The States Attorney did call a Grand Jury to deliberate on five of the seven men I had stopped. I was called to testify. I faced about five separate attorneys who worked for the defendants. I recall one attorney asked me why I thought his client was at the riot. This attorney worked for the man who had been hit with something like a two by four on his ear. I thought his question was pretty stupid. I got to explain the cars being parked at King Tuts, his client trying to flee the arriving car to his own vehicle, his clients bleeding ear, and the union t-shirts. Despite what evidence we had, as far as I know, there were not any successful prosecutions in the case.

If justice was served here, it was monetary justice. I spoke to one of the attorneys on the case. He claimed each of the defendants had been required to put up a $150,000 retainer for his lawyer. He indicated the Labor Union had put the retainer money up for the defendants. That would mean the defense (Union) paid $150,000 times five defendants which would be $750,000. Rioting sure costs money!!!!

Clarification: I have been a Union member all of my working life. I have been in the United Auto Workers, United Mine workers and Illinois Teachers Association. I have also belonged to the Federation of Police (FOP) which calls itself a lodge but works very similar to a union. Regardless of my Union leanings, as I am pro-union, there is no place for violence in union activities.

CHAPTER 70
THE SERGEANT WHO COULD NOT SHOOT STRAIGHT

When a person decides to become a police officer, he/she should examine themselves and see if they have the required personality and skills to do the job. For example, if a person cannot tell others 'No" and mean it they should never become a cop. Telling others they must stop a certain behavior is a key personality trait each officer must possess. An underrated skill is running. While not used often, sometimes the police must run down fleeing suspects. An inability to run could mean a murderer escapes. One skill that is paramount above all others and that is shooting. While shooting is rarely utilized, it is so important when needed. An officer who can shoot well is able to protect his own life as well as others in a shooting situation. This is a story about a Sergeant who lacked shooting skills.

I went through the Illinois State Police Academy and had a full forty hours of handgun and shotgun training. Some of the older cops who were still working in 1987 had received no academy training. Some of the older officers had been sent to do mobile team training. (this is where a group of officers meet at a site close to where they work and the training team comes to them and puts on training) I am not sure how thorough such training was as some of the older officers were just to put it plainly "bad shooters."

When I arrived at my first post in E. St. Louis, my Sergeant was nearing the end of his career and had probably been trained by a mobile team. The Sergeant was the highest ranking officer in E. St Louis. The Sergeant's bosses were the Lieutenant and Captain and they were fifty miles away in Mt Vernon, Illinois. Needless to say I did not want to upset the Sergeant.

On our first shoot, the old Sergeant lined up beside me. I graded his shooting and he graded mine. We were shooting at bulls eyes targets with a 7 point ring being the lowest score you could receive. The targets then had a 8 point ring, a 9 point ring, and a bulls eye, which was worth 10 points. The Sergeant was missing all the rings and on some of his better shots he managed to hit the white area that was outside all the rings.

I was correctly scoring the white area outside the rings as zero points. Old Sarge saw his zeros on his scorecard and was very upset with me. Sarge insisted when he hit the target outside the numbered rings he should receive a 6 on his scorecard.

I explained I had just returned from the academy and any shot outside the rings gives the shooter zero points. I said it is like missing the bad guy in a gunfight. A shot into the white on a target is a worthless shot.

Old Sarge got his dander up. Those are six point shots and I order you to make them sixes.

I took my pen out and changed each zero to a six. Without the sixes Sarge would have failed the shoot.

After I got to know him well I use to kid the old Sergeant. I told him if he was ever in a real gunfight to throw the gun at the bad guy and run. There would be at least some chance the thrown gun would do some damage.

CHAPTER 71
THE SNEEZER

As I got to the close of my career as a police officer, I received a promotion to a Commercial Motor Vehicle Officer (CVEO). The job came with a large pay raise and lots of overtime. This job with its high pay scale and overtime arguably made me the highest paid State Police officer in the district. The down side to the position was that I was required to be available for call outs at any time of the night. If a large truck were involved in a crash, I was called out to determine the mechanical state of the truck and fitness of the driver involved.

On the night of this story, I was sleeping at 4 A.M. when the phone rang. I was told a semi-tractor trailer hauling a tanker trailer had hit a truck parked on the roadway edge on I57 at the West Frankfort, Illinois exit Northbound.

I arrived within minutes of the call and the fire department was using the Jaws of Life to cut an older woman out of the passenger seat of an old pickup truck. The old lady was hollering about her husband. Since the driver's seat of the pickup was unoccupied, I asked the firemen where the driver was at. The firemen did not know. The old woman said he was in the camper changing his underwear.

The pickup had been hit in the rear by an 80,000 pound semi-truck driving 70 miles per hour. There was no camper shell anywhere in view. A search party began to look for the camper shell. Finally a fireman yelled he had located the shell.

The shell appeared to me to be a football field North and slightly East of the accident site. Upon getting to the shell, we discovered the little old man inside the collapsed camper shell. With some pulling and bending, the firemen rescued the little guy and shipped him off to the hospital,

The driver of the semi would not admit to going to sleep. It was obvious to me he drifted off and then lined himself up on what he believed to be a moving vehicle in front of him. Unfortunately, the truck ahead of him was off the road and a little old man was changing his underwear in the camper. "Boom" he hits a parked vehicle.

The driver would not admit to going to sleep. Evidently he knew going to sleep was against the law, so he kept saying he was sneezing multiple times and went off the road and hit the parked truck. In the very same statue that says drivers cannot fall asleep without pulling off the road it says if they are ill they must pull off the road. I cited the driver for improper lane usage and driving while ill (something caused him to sneeze).

I feel some important lessons were learned in this crash. The driver of the semi learned that sneezing is not any better excuse for hitting a parked vehicle than sleeping. The driver of the pickup and his wife learned never to pull over to the interstate edge in the middle of the night and change underwear.

CHAPTER 72
THE TERRORIST

Terrorism is a big problem for this country. Terrorist intend to put "terror" into the population in order to alter the governments behavior or to bring about the governments demise. Terrorists come in all flavors. What I mean is, they can be from the far left and want to abolish animal research or be from the far right and want less government. Certainly we are familiar with jihadist terrorism. The jihadist wants to abolish our government because we are not the right religion. They wish for a government that uses sharia law. Catching a terrorist probably ranks high on every State policeman's wish list and I actually caught one.

I was working a late evening shift and it was summer time and very hot. I had removed my bullet proof vest due to the heat. Things had not been going my way this evening. As a cop working at a scale, too often things happen that is beyond our control. The truck weigh inspectors only write overweight citations in Illinois. Those truck weigh inspectors often get suspended drivers or wanted persons or discover bad equipment as they do their jobs. They then hand those problems off to the trooper working the scale, which in this case is me. All these unplanned issues were about to make me miss my evening meal. I finally got a break and headed to supper.

I left the scale not bothering on put on my vest thinking I was going straight to the diner for a good meal. I no more than cleared the scale and I noticed a car off to the side of the road in the emergency stop lane. Now I wanted to ignore the car and go on to the diner. If I ignored the car, I took the chance someone was having a heart attack or some other calamity. I did not want that to happen so I stopped.

I went up and noticed the driver's car had overheated. He (the driver) was in the driver's seat and I asked for his driver's license. The man did obviously not want to give me what I had asked for. He fiddled around and denied having a driver's license or any paperwork, like a social security card.

I was getting the feeling I sometimes get when things aren't quite right. It was a sense of danger. I would get this feeling about twice a year. It was as if the hair was standing up on my neck, followed by an adrenaline dump. You feel like fighting of fleeing. I recall thinking I sure wish I had put my bullet proof vest back on.

I ordered the guy from his car and felt his back pocket. It contained a wallet so I pulled it out. I found an old driver's license. I put him back in his car and went to my squad car.

I did a computer driver's license check on him. I was told this guy was a terrorist with a federal warrant on him for terrorism. Now I had a dilemma. Do I stand by and wait for assistance or do I try to take him into custody by myself.

I decided to try to do it by myself. I knew he did not have a gun on his person as I had already searched him to get the driver's license. I knew he could have a gun in the car but I had looked fairly close on my first trip to his car and did not see one. This was a calculated gamble and I knew it. I pulled my pistol out and had in my hand but laid it down by the side of my right leg as I walked back to his car.

I ordered the guy out and had him face away from me. I holstered my gun and got handcuffs on the terrorist.

I got the guy to my squad car and buckled him in the seat belt. We began to talk. This guy was a Timothy McVeigh type of terrorist. He was from the far right and wanted to overthrow the U.S. government and get back to the freedoms he felt the country's earlier forefathers knew. I wasn't overly impressed with his intelligence and doubt if he could produce a bomb like McVeigh did at the federal building in Oklahoma City Oklahoma that killed so many people.

The guy did strike me as a killer. I could see the killer mentality in his attitude toward government in general and me in particular. I was thankful all had gone as well as it did. He stated he felt he had just messed up. He wished he had fought me and fled.

As we talked, I had a crazy idea occurred to me. I could catch a killer here, if he is willing to talk. I could end up as a Trooper who solved several murders. I could end up doing an episode on the ID channel.

I asked, "Have you ever killed anybody."

"Why would I tell you if I have killed someone?" He asked.

I explained he was going away to prison probably for the rest of his life. I said this was his chance to get it all off his chest. I also argued that in prison there is a certain status that comes with the reputation of being a murderer.

This terrorist said, I ain't telling you nothing."

I am convinced the terrorist reply says it all. He did not say he had not killed anyone and I believed he did at some point. He also made it clear he would not cooperate with a government agent like me.

Too bad I did not get any cooperation. I sure would like to have had an episode on the ID channel 1!

CHAPTER 73
THE UNSCRUPULOUS CORONER

Being an unscrupulous person does not always involve doing something illegal. One of my relatives was known for feeling it was alright to take others money when they had made an accounting error. He would go to the bank and if in the course of a transaction a teller gave him cash above the amount he should have received, he considered the extra cash his own good fortune. When asked about taking what should have been the banks money, he would reply that the bank should have hired more competent tellers. He would also say the bank had plenty of money that they had ripped people off of and they were just getting some of their own medicine. My relative had not stolen the money but he certainly had not considered the poor teller who had made an innocent error. My relative also did not consider how the poor teller would now have the repay the bank from their personal money. This story is about a questionable Corner. This Corner did not do anything illegal but I find his actions unscrupulous.

The story starts late one evening in Herrin, Illinois. It was about 12 midnight and I was patrolling Il Rt 148 or Park Avenue. I was at one of the many red lights of Park Avenue and had stopped behind a large Harley motorcycle. The light turned green and the Harley rider simply fell over on his motorcycle. I put my overhead lights on and went to help the forty year old man pick up his motorcycle. My thinking was that Harleys are pretty heavy and this guy had momentarily let his motorcycle's weight become off balance and had fallen over. When I got the motorcycle up righted, I realized this guy had spent too much time at the bar; he was intoxicated.

I arrested the motorcycle rider for driving while intoxicated. I towed his motorcycle. I gave him multiple citations and his warning to motorist. The warning to motorist was very important as it allowed the motorcyclist to drive for the next 45 days before a suspension set in and he could no longer legally drive. I released the man to go home after he provided me with the required bond.

Two nights later I get called to Il Rt. 148 approximately four miles South of Herrin Illinois. I was told this was a car/motorcycle crash and the motorcycle driver is possibly dead. I race to the scene. A car, driven by a young woman, was passing another car. The pass was taking place on a very elevated road (i.e. 15 to 20 feet above the surrounding bottom land). The road was designed with barricades on both sides to prevent cars from plunging off the road into the wooded bottom land down below. The woman had plowed head on into a motorcycle. The poor motorcyclist was unable to get away from the oncoming car as he had nowhere to go. The barricades prevented his leaving the roadway without being ejected off the cycle, being airborne at 20 feet or so above the woods, where he would have ultimately landed. So the biker hit the lady's car head on and was thrown a good distance before landing on the road.

I checked the biker's pulse and he was dead. I called for an accident reconstructionist and had to await their arrival before I could move the dead bilker. A sergeant arrived and helped me block off the roadway so as to preserve the integrity of the crash scene.

Since there was no traffic entering our area my Sergeant and I began to talk. I told him I felt sure I knew this biker but could not place how I knew him. I was not able to turn him over until photos were taken and I could not see his face. Finally my memory began to work, I told the Sergeant this dead man was someone I had arrest for DUI two days earlier. The Sergeant did not believe me. In time I searched the dead man's rear pockets. Sure enough the biker's pocket contained all my citations and warning to motorist he had received two days earlier.

Finally the Coroner arrived in the County's coroners van. The Coroner went through the normal procedure of declaring the man dead and putting an official time on his date of death. We loaded up the body on a gurney and placed it in the Coroner's van. The Coroner asked me to go with him on the death notice to the family. I agreed to go with him.

In route to the dead man's home, I asked the Coroner if we should change vehicles. I was concerned the family would realize their loved one was inside and chaos would result. The Coroner said he did this often and families don't think to look in the van. He explained their grief would be such that they would not consider the van as having their loved on inside. Well the good Corner had more experience in this than I did so off we went.

We arrived at the dead man's home and the Coroner told the dead man's mother and middle school child of the loss of their son and father. The mother went to wailing and crying the child kind of sat around in disbelief. Then the Coroner got off base. He explained he owned a funeral home and if the family did not know where they wanted to send the body he would be glad to do the funeral for them.

I am convinced no laws were broken. Perhaps the Coroner meant well by offering a service to a distraught family. But since the Coroner was the a public official perhaps a little digression would have been in order... Don't offer your services as a funeral home director while doing Coroner duties!

CHAPTER 74
THE WRONG SIDE OF THE RAILROAD TRACKS

When I was young, my mother often talked of people who were unfortunate enough to be "born on the wrong side of the railroad tracks." This statement meant that the unlucky person being referred to had done nothing wrong but had been born into a bad situation. The person spoken of would be unlikely to ever be made right in the eyes of society. For example, a girl might be born very poor and never learn proper grammar due to her family's speech habits and her having to leave school early to go to work to help support her brothers and sisters. This is a story of my "being from the wrong side of the tracks."

I was employed with the Illinois Commerce Commission Police in 1994. Our job was to regulate trucking in Illinois. We made sure the companies hauling the freight within our borders had the proper licenses and had paid the proper governmental fees. A federal court case took place and our jobs were to be eliminated. I was told my job would soon be terminated and I took a leave of absence from the State of Illinois and went to work as an underground coal miner. While working in the mine, I received a phone call from my former Illinois Commerce Commission Police boss. I was told that many Illinois Commerce Commission Police were going to be allowed to become Illinois State Police Troopers. I was asked if I would like to test to become a Trooper.

I tested successfully for a position of Illinois State Trooper and was sent to the Illinois State Police Academy. I spent 14 weeks as a cadet. Being a cadet is very similar to being in the Army's boot camp. Forced runs of seven miles occurred along with many pushups and other discipline techniques. What made my personal cadet program so difficult is that this was my second go round of this boot camp type atmosphere. I had already done 16 weeks of academy work in 1987 when the State of Illinois Secretary of State Police hired me.

When I came to the District 13 as a Trooper, I was surprised that I had come from the "wrong side of the tracks" in the mind of many of my fellow Troopers. Many Troopers from District 13 felt I had come from the Illinois Commerce Commission Police and had not applied directly to the Troopers and therefore was an "unfit Trooper." This idea really bothered me since I had actually done more academy time than any of these fellows.

What happened next surprised me further. Several of the Troopers seldom would speak with me. Some or perhaps one of them evidently filled my mailbox with trash. Someone would take items form my mailbox. A Master Sergeant came to me after I handled my first fatal crash and said several of the Troops were hoping I would fail at my job.

Several years later, I thought the whole affair was over. Some of the most vocal critics of my being a Trooper had retired. I had been made a Commercial Motor Vehicle Inspector with the Troopers. I was examining trucks to see if they were safe to allow on Illinois roadways. Part of my examination was to check hazardous material trucks. I was to be sure no hazardous material was spilling on the roadway.

I found a truck one night that appeared to be leaking class 8 corrosive materials. This corrosive material would burn the skin off a human being if it were to come into contact with anyone. The material was so corrosive that it might well have burned the tires off any vehicle that drove across it.

I placed the truck out of service at the far end of the truck weigh scale parking lot and forced the trucking company hauling the material to call out a specialist to deal with the leak. The problem is I was wrong. The night I found the truck in question was a cool fall evening. The hot corrosive material had caused condensation to form on the bottom of the tanker trailer. What I thought was dangerous hazardous material was simply water (condensation).

When word got out that I had placed a perfectly good trailer out of service at least two of my fellow Troopers seemed pleased of my failure. These two had always been critics of my having become a Trooper from the Illinois Commerce Commission Police.

I was disheartened. I expected to be written up (a form of punishment) for my failure in placing the truck out of service. I was disappointed the old "he came from the wrong side of the tracks issue had reappeared."

Sure enough the Master Sergeant called saying he needed to speak to me concerning the placing of the hazmat trailer out of service when it was perfectly fine. When the Master Sergeant arrived, I braced for the worst. The Master Sergeant brought out a letter from the trucking company I had injured by causing them the cost of the expert (who found the load was fine) and down time on their load delivery. The Master Sergeant read the letter. The letter from the company said I was an asset to the Illinois State Police Troopers. The letter read I was doing a great job protecting the citizens on my great state. The Master Sergeant said he was placing the letter in my file and to keep up the great work.

I was stunned. I expected to be reprimanded and instead was praised. The two Troopers, who were gleeful at my mess up, were as stunned as I was. I could see them shaking their heads in disbelief. One of the two even commented he could not believe I received a letter of commendation on a screw up.

The whole hazmat incident seemed to change things. I was accepted as a legitimate Trooper, even by the two listed critics, from that day on. I guess you could say I was no longer from the "wrong side of the tracks."

CHAPTER 75
TRACKING THE SUSPECT IN A CEMETERY

The Illinois State police do not teach any "tracking" classes. Tracking probably hasn't been taught since the 1800' by the Texas Rangers. If someone runs away from a traffic stop, police most often simply call in a canine to do the tracking. This case (plus one other) is unusual in that I tracked the suspect.

On one snowy night I received a radio call from Illinois State Police headquarters in Du Quoin that a State Truck had been struck on Il Rt 37 near Marion Illinois. I drove to the scene and a State Truck had been plowing snow had been struck in the rear by a car. The car was running and its driver's side door was open. The truck operator was still in his truck. I opened the truck door and asked where the driver of the car was. I was expecting to be told he had gone to the hospital or had ducked into the skating rink that was nearby due to the cold. The driver of the truck said the car driver had taken off running across a large cemetery located to our East.

I could see the suspect's footprints in the snow and began to run through the cemetery following them. Since few people flee accidents, I was reasonably sure something was amiss here. I pulled my pistol as I ran. I got to the last footprint and it appeared my suspect had been "beamed up" like in a star wars movie. There was a last step then no further footprints.

I don't believe in being "beamed up" but I was perplexed. I stopped and listened. My suspect was a heavy man and the run through the snow had winded him. I could hear his heave breathing behind a mausoleum. The suspect had evidently seen me running across the cemetery and realized I was going to overtake him. He had taken his last step at running and then had jumped to a position behind the mausoleum.

I ordered the suspect out from behind the mausoleum. I got him handcuffed. I escorted him a good block back to my squad car. I pulled an old wallet from his pants and ran a computer warrant check on him. My suspect was an escapee from the Indiana prison system. He had escaped about a year earlier.

On the way to the jail the suspect began to beg me to let him go. He said he had finally found a good woman and they had a new baby. He wept as he told me had made a new life and was going straight.

When we got to the jail, I told the suspect he would do well to quit crying. I reminded him jail is a tough place and crying would only bring him derision and perhaps get him beat up. I wiped his tears off his face and gave him time to compose himself.

I took the suspect to the jail. This was an old jail and when you arrived via an elevator (the jail was on the third floor) there were two holding cells side by side ahead of you. An officer had to search the suspect one last time in front of the two holding cells. Then the handcuffs were removed and all the suspect's belongings were put in the jailers care. Then you took the suspect around a corner, which was still in hearing distance of the prisoners in the holding cells, to do fingerprinting.

As I filled out my fingerprint card, I would ask the suspect his height, weight, hair color, eye color etc. This guy had gone from crying to acting tough for the holding cell inmates. So when I asked his height he said F*** You. I guessed his height and then asked him his weight at which I got the same response. I leaned over and whispered in his ear "Do that again and I'm going to tell those holding cell inmates you cried all the way to jail". I asked him again his weight and he replied "270 pounds sir. " Problem solved.

CHAPTER 76
TRAINING DAY AND THE BAD SERGEANT

When I first became an Illinois State Trooper, training was something that was taken seriously at the academy but not something that was serious at the District. After graduating from the academy, a Troopers training day at the district was pretty much a fun day. The Troopers would mingle and tell stories but he training was almost worthless. Then the shooting incident at Columbine High School in Colorado occurred. Now things changed.

The first change was the way we handled an active shooter situation. In the past, when we had a hostage situation, all arriving Troopers would establish a perimeter. A perimeter was an area around the shooting sight in which no one was allowed in and no one went out of without permission. Neighbors or people in the perimeter were checked and moved to a safer location. A negotiator was called in to try to talk the shooter into surrendering. A swat team was placed around the perimeter that had been established by the first arriving Troopers. A swat team would charge the shooter when all other means had been exhausted. After the shooting at Columbine, all the above changed. Police realized that mass shooters had no intent on surrendering and for police to wait and negotiate meant more lives would be lost than if we charged in as soon as we arrived.

Our District command decided to go all out on the new training. The district command found an old Greek fraternity house on Southern Illinois University's campus that had been condemned and was abandoned. The house had multiple rooms and state employees were brought in from other districts to play victims and hostage takers. We were armed with paint guns. The guns had what appeared to be a 22 caliber gas firing paint bullet. These bullets were designed not to kill but to mark accuracy. If a trooper decided to shoot someone, the paint of the bullet would mark the person shot. After the situation was played out, success or failure depended on shooting the right person and shooting them well enough to end the hostage takers ability to function.

The Troopers were put into teams at random. A person from within the Greek house would scream, and blank guns would be shot, to create the illusion of a hostage being killed. The troopers would rush into the Greek house being guided by the screams and gunshots. Actors would grab at you claiming to be victims and begging for help. The actors would have fake blood all over them. Other actors would be employed to be bad guys waiting to kill you as you entered the building. The entering Trooper team had to get beyond the wounded and get to the killer; all the while shooting only bad guys as they proceeded to the primary shooter.

We had a Sergeant that was known for being a stickler for following detail. The Sergeant (acting as a bad guy) had placed himself in the hallway we would be using to race to the primary shooter. He had his own paint gun to shoot up the Trooper team and was hidden in a closet in that hallway. As the team came very fast toward the primary shooter, the Sergeant jumps out behind our team. I was a rear guard with this team and the Sergeant jumps out in front of me. I let him have it with the paint gun. I knew I got him with the first few rounds and if it was anybody else I would have quit firing. I knew this guy was a stickler for detail so I felt I had to keep firing to make absolutely sure there was no question he was properly shot with paint that he could not later say he was only wounded.

The problem for the Sergeant was these paint balls really hurt. From close range the paint balls will take your breath away. I was shooting this guy at point blank range over and over. After shooting him about ten rounds, he screams out to please stop.

Later I saw the Sergeants chest. The Sergeants chest looked like he had been stung by a hive of bees. The good part of this is I exceeded expectations on properly killing the Sergeant. The down side is I think he was a little upset I pumped ten rounds of paint balls into his chest at point blank range. Oh well, all in a day's work.

CHAPTER 77
TRYING TO FIND MY OVERWEIGHT SCALES

Illinois has laws regarding how much weight can be on a given road. The laws are designed to protect the roadway surface from cracking and becoming full of potholes. Potholes and cracks cost big money on road repair, so trucks are allowed only a certain amount of weight on an axle and a certain amount on the whole truck. Better roads can carry more weight than poorly made roads. Truck drivers know that the class of a road determines how much weight the truck can carry. Some roads in Illinois are 73,280 pound roads and some are good for 80,000 pounds. If a truck owner wants his trucks to carry more weight than allowed, he must prove a need to violate the weight laws and then buy an expensive permit. The permit money then goes in to a fund to repair the road at a later date.

To catch overweight trucks, the Illinois State Police assigns certain troopers to go and look for them. I would receive the overweight truck detail about every six or eight weeks. Finding an overweight truck is quite a skill. Most trucks are legally operated and finding an overweight one is tough. Some loads of over-sized material (i.e. a Bulldozer) are overweight and are worth stopping but most often the driver has an overweight permit. Other loads appear to be legal loads (i.e. like a grain trailer) but are very overweight. I discovered that a truck with flattened of tires (due to the load) on side roads was the clearest indicator of an overweight truck.

Once I discovered what appeared to be an overweight truck I would stop the unit. I would ask to see the bill of laden (paperwork) for the load. Sometimes the paperwork would show the load to be of legal weight. Other times the trucker would try to provide me with an earlier bill of laden in which his weight was legal and then hide the bill of laden for the present load. Still other times the driver would claim there was not a bill of laden given him when he picked up the load.

If I could determine from the bill of laden the truck was within legal limits, I would let the driver proceed. If I could not determine the truck to be of legal weight, I would get on my police radio and call for my Henry van. The Henry van was just a white van with no markings that carried the portable scales and a printout machine to provide proof of the trucks actual weight.

A Henry van was supposed to shadow me with the driver not allowing the van to seen by the truck drivers. Usually the van would hide in a cemetery or somewhere close to my location, while I searched for the overweight truck. Once I found an overweight truck, I would call for the van and it would arrive quickly. We would place the portable scales under the trucks tires and literally weigh the entire truck. The whole weighing process could be done in minutes.

The problem I was encountering was a reluctant Henry van driver. The van driver liked to consort with another trooper and would often be talking when I needed him. He simply would not answer his radio.

I spoke to the Henry van driver about this and could not seem to change his behavior. I thought about reporting him to his supervisors but really did not want to do this. I remembered that the Henry van driver's wife ran a company that had a truck. Ah yes my problems could be solved.

The next time I was near where the Henry vans drivers wife's truck was close I stopped a truck. When I called for the Henry van I got no answer. So I went out and found the truck belonging to the Henry van driver's wife. I escorted the van to a permanent scale on 157. Sure enough the Henry van driver's wife's truck was overweight. The Henry van driver was furiously calling me saying he was available to help me. I said I really don't need you now as I have escorted a truck to the scale.

I think I cured two problems that day. I got an overweight truck off the road and cured the Henry van driver from ignoring my calls for assistance.

CHAPTER 78
TWO DUI ARRESTS AND STAYING ETHICAL

A DUI arrest is a time consuming and difficult arrest. The officer must find the DUI and make a traffic stop. Once the officer sees signs of excessive alcohol intake by the suspect, he/she must take the suspect through a series of field sobriety test. If the suspect fails the test, he/she is handcuffed. A tow truck is called and an inventory of the car is done. The suspect is transported to a police station which has a breath alcohol machine. The suspect receives a citation for whatever the stop started from (i.e. illegal lane usage, no taillight, etc) and for DUI. The suspect is then read a warning to motorist, which explains the penalty failure to blow in the machine (i.e. six months suspension of driving privileges). A twenty minute wait ensues, where the officer makes sure the suspect does not belch up alcohol into their mouth (which would invalidate the breath test). Finally the breath test if offered. If the test shows the suspect is DUI a third citation is written for being DUI above the .08 threshold. The suspect is given a paper showing how long they can legally drive before the DUI suspension kicks in. Finally the report of all the officer and defendants actions is completed. If everything goes right this process takes three and a half hours of nonstop work.

On the night in question I started my shift about 6 P.M. I found my first drunk about 6:30 P.M. and went through the above process. By 10 P.M. I left the Franklin county jail. I was exhausted as I pulled onto Il Rt 34 from the courthouse. I drove three blocks toward the Benton, Illinois square and had a car pull in front of me to make a left turn. The car did not use it's blinker and I turned right to follow it. The car pulled into a one way street going the wrong direction. The car parked directly in front of a bar. I activated my lights and walked to the car.

A young woman was driving the car and had her husband beside her. The woman was well dressed but seemed difficult as she wanted me to go away as she was going to the bar. I looked inside the car and saw open containers of beer for both her and her husband. I decided to work with the husband first and gave him a citation for illegal transportation of alcohol by a passenger.

As I was writing this citation, a close personal friend of mine appeared at my squad car window. The friend asked me to roll down my window. I complied and listened to what my friend had to say. The friend said this lady was a good friend of his. He explained the lady was an outstanding member of the community and could I give her a break. I replied "thank you for telling me of your friend but I must do my job."

I was having an ethical dilemma. While I thought this woman would turn out to be DUI, I was not yet sure. I was tired from having completed one DUI arrest tonight already. My friend was asking for this lady a break. If I let her go to the bar, I was kind of covered as she would be there for several hours and if she got popped for DUI later I would be off the hook since she did in fact go to a bar. Unfortunately I was really considering this.

I took the husbands citation to the car. I explained the citation to him and prepared to deal with his wife. The wife beats me to the punch as she wants to deal with me. She says, "did you write my husband a ticket."

I said yes mam, I did.

At my reply the lady says, "I'll see your ass in court."

My ethical dilemma was over. Within a few minutes, we had gone through the field sobriety test and she had failed as badly as I had expected her to. So she received her earned DUI and got to see me in court too.

As for my friend, he should have never asked for a break for the woman. He should have understood I had a job to do. I did not see my friend for several years after this event. When we met, I explained how his intervention bothered me. Surprisingly he now agreed he should have not got involved with this traffic stop.

CHAPTER 79
UNCLE BILL AND UNCLE JERRY

    Everybody has relatives they enjoy more than others. I personally enjoy being around relatives who don't put on airs. That is to say, they act down to earth and don't pretend to be overly important. People like this make good company. I have always enjoyed being in my Uncle Jerry's company. Jerry is actually not my relative at all but comes from my wife's side of the family. Jerry is a straight forward guy. Jerry also has the great gift of being a good listener. Perhaps the reason I like Jerry most is that he likes a good cop story. When we get together, he would often ask for a cop story. Without giving Jerry any names, I would give him the broad outline of an arrest I had recently made. The stories Jerry enjoyed are the same ones I am telling you with this book.

    Well I had told Jerry an interesting story of a really dumb criminal. The story began when I had observed a car without proper registration at an intersection. I went forward and spoke to the driver and asked for his license and insurance card. The young man provided me the necessary information and I performed a computer driver's license check on him. The check showed the young man was in fact driving while suspended. I went forward and asked the young man if he had the required $100.00 in cash bond for driving while suspended. He said he did not have bond and I handcuffed him and put him in my squad car.

    I got in my car and was preparing to order a tow truck to take away the car when the young man began to ask questions. The young man asked if I had to tow his car. I said if I took him away from his car I would have to tow it. I said I could not leave it on a parking lot as I would be responsible if it were damaged. I said it was a shame he lacked bond because if he had the required bond, I would let him call a friend and stay with his car and save himself a tow bill.

I could see the young man was considering something but I was unsure what it could be. Finally he says, "if you jerk on the console, it comes up, and I have $100.00 hidden there." Then in the next breath he says "no forget it, I will go to jail."

I said, "stay calm, relax, it's not that much trouble, I will get your money and keep you from having to go to jail."

I go to the car and pull on the console. Sure enough the console comes up. Sure enough there is the money. Problem is this is where the young man kept his cannabis.

I go back to my squad car. I explain that yes I found the $100.00 in cash for bond. The problem is that the young man now needs two hundred dollars. He needed one hundred for driving while suspended and one hundred for possessing the cannabis. The young man lacked the required bond and his car was towed and he went to jail for lacking sufficient bond.

Jerry liked the story and howled with laughter.

Several weeks after I told Jerry the cop story, he calls me. Jerry's says his brother, Uncle Bill is moving from one home to another. Jerry says he needs help with picking up and moving the heavy articles like couches and chairs. I show up and several other young men are assisting.

We get the job done and are taking a break. Jerry says, "John, tell us a cop story." I have recognized the young man in the above story as one of the furniture movers. I explain to Jerry I'm all out of cop stories. I am sure this gang of young men has many cop stories they could tell on themselves. Thus they would not be interested in a cop story.

To my horror Jerry says I have a good cop story. Jerry begins to tell the story on the guy I arrested who kept his drugs under his console. The guy I arrested knows it is him the story is about. The arrestee doesn't let on and I don't either. The rest of the gang is unaware of who is being spoken of. Other than the arrestee and I being embarrassed the day finishes well.

Good ole Uncle Jerry!

CHAPTER 80
WAS IT TERRORISM?

As I sit here writing this story, a terrorist attack has just taken place in Nice, France. Eighty four people were run over by a jihad terrorist driving a truck. While terrorist up till now seem to prefer bullets and airplanes as instruments of terror, I suspected the use of a truck would be coming soon. The reason I thought a truck would be used is based on this story.

It was about 2003 when I was called to a truck wreck at the I57 southbound rest area in Franklin County. When I arrived, I could see a truck tractor semi-trailer had hit a small tree and it completely flipped the truck onto its top. The rest areas restrooms would have been struck had the small tree not have flipped the truck. The rest area was very crowded due to being a Friday night in the summertime.

The driver was dead. He was trapped in his seat belt and was hanging upside down. The driver had been killed by a loose citizens band radio. The radio should have been bolted to the truck so it would not fly around the cab of the truck in an accident. Since this c.b. radio was placed in a slot above the driver's head, it came flying out when the truck overturned and lodged in the driver's forehead. The passenger was injured but alive. We cut the passenger out of his seat belt and used a helicopter to fly him off to a trauma unit in St. Louis, Missouri. I was able to grab the passenger's driver's license before he was flown away to the hospital.

I checked with a few witnesses who were standing around and they described the truck as deliberating accelerating up the ramp coming off the interstate. These ramps are designed to allow vehicles to slow down before coming into the parking area of the rest stop. I was surprised at this information and began to wonder if the gas pedal of the truck had stuck. One witness said that could not be true as you could hear the driver shifting into a higher gear to gain more speed. All the witnesses indicated that had the truck struck the rest areas rest room building multiple people (estimated about 20 to 40) would have died.

I looked at the trucks mechanical system and the brakes worked. The gas feed had not stuck. Nothing mechanically on the truck would have caused this accident. The accident was either caused by driver error or it was an intentional attack.

I looked at the driver's license of the man who was driving the truck, and compared it with the passenger's driver's license. Both men were originally Pakistani and their names were very long. One letter was added to the truck operator's driver's license that made it different from the passenger's driver's license. Both men were listed as being born on the same year and the same day. Both men had the exact same address in Ontario, Canada.

I phoned the trucking company in Canada, who owned the truck and semi-trailer. I gave them the truck unit number so they could use the computer to locate their company information. Then I told them their driver was dead but the co-driver had been flown to St. Louis Missouri.

The dispatcher of the trucking company abruptly said I must be mistaken. The dispatcher said this was a solo unit and there was no co-driver. They asked the name and date of birth of the driver. When I supplied the name and date of birth of the driver, the dispatcher said I had added an extra letter to the driver's name.

I explained the man the dispatcher had said was their driver was in fact the passenger today. I reiterated that the man they were calling their driver was in St Louis, Missouri.

The Canadian company had no record of the actual driver on their payroll. They were unaware he was on the truck. They did not know anyone but their employee was supposed to be on this truck.

What I had here was a driver who is living with the passenger at the same address in Canada. The drivers name was within a letter of matching the passengers name and their date of birth was the same. This driver was deliberately speeding toward a rest stop restroom with about 20 to 40 people in and around it. The only thing that prevented this catastrophe was a small tree. This tree would not have stopped a slow moving truck but flipped the fast moving unit. The driver might have caused more trouble but was killed by a c.b. set to the head. The passenger was incapacitated.

I felt at the time this was a terrorist attack but could not get my superiors to look further into it with Canadian authorities. The passenger survived and could do further terrorism in the future if not detected. Oh well I did my best.

CHAPTER 81
WHAT? A DRUNKEN GRANDMA!

In my career as a State Policeman, I did hundreds of DUI arrest. Men comprised about two thirds of my arrest and women about a third. Women who were intoxicated were more problematic than men. Sometimes they would try to be sexy, other times argumentative, but once they were sure they were going to jail, they were hateful. Men had issues too but more often times than not the man would accept his fate and not give me too much trouble. I seldom had older drunks (over 65 years of age). In fact I only remember three older drunks. The three fell into my usual pattern; two men (2/3) and one woman (1/3). This is a story of the older woman.

Good drunks that try to hide their alcoholism always drink vodka. While most alcoholic drinks leave a distinctive odor, vodka does not. So vodka drinkers put their vodka in soda containers or other non-alcoholic containers and carry that container around all day. The rest of society is often unaware of the person's inebriated state. The better disguisers develop pretty good coordination. Although legally drunk (over .08 percent blood alcohol level), the disguiser can walk and talk fairly well. Though disguised, these people still have trouble multitasking. A person, who is DUI, will have trouble doing two things at once; which is why we have them count while standing on one leg. The drunk can stand or count but not stand and count. This is why even good drunks have trouble driving. If something distracts them, they cannot control the car.

My story begins on a peaceful summer afternoon. I receive a dispatch to go to Skyline drive about three miles South of Marion, Illinois. I arrived to find a car had run off the right side (passenger side) of the roadway and flipped on its side. The driver was an older female, around 68 years of age. The woman was not injured but was just shaken up over her accident. I looked at the accident scene and tried to make sense of it. The lady admitted to falling off the roadway and trying to jerk the car back over the asphalt shoulder. She said she was not run off the road by another vehicle. She said she did not swerve to avoid an animal.

I looked at her. She was somebody's grandma. It was early afternoon so it was not a normal time to have a DUI on the road. The lady's speech was clear. Still this crash made no sense as it was on a straight section of road which had no issues like rain or ice on it. So I got my portable breath tester out and bingo….this woman is very drunk.

I could not let the lady do the walk and turn test or one leg stand test as she was too old and heavy. I checked her eyes and she clearly had horizontal gaze nystagmus. Her eyes followed the pen I held in front of her face and then when I stopped with the pen before paralleling her shoulders, her eyes had a violent twitching (nystagmus). I informed the lady she was intoxicated and she admitted drinking vodka today.

I told the woman she was under arrest and she got hateful. She said I had just cost her a 26 year marriage as her husband did not know she drank. No amount of reasoning would convince this woman that she was responsible for her own drinking and marriage.

Well I took the old drunken woman to jail. She got her husband to bail her out. I think this lady's husband learned something. I am sure his eyes were opened to why she was so volatile in the marriage. Me... I learned that even grandma can be DUI.

CHAPTER 82
WOMAN SETS DAUGHTER STRAIGHT AFTER DUI

    The modern assumption is that "we all want to be good parents". Some of the people I met must have been raised by coyotes as they just did not seem to understand parenting. These peoples' parenting skills were so bad I figured they were not properly given love and attention as they grew up. This is a short story to illustrate my point.

    It was Super Bowl Sunday in February somewhere around the year 2000. I was driving in Herrin, Illinois. I was traveling down a side street called 14th Street. As I come to an intersection, a green car runs the stop sign and almost strikes my squad car. I put my squad in reverse and get back far enough to get behind the stop sign violator. I activate my lights and the green car stops abruptly. I go forward and the driver of the green car is a 30ish year old white female.

    I take the lady through the field sobriety test and she is plastered. The odor of her breath gives me the belief she has been guzzling beer and watching the game, probably at a local bar. I arrest her and she is complaining she is going to be in trouble with her employer which is a local church.

    I get the lady to the county jail and she says she must pee. I get the county matron to assist her in using the bathroom. When the lady returns from the bathroom, I start my 20 minute watch to make sure she has not belched alcohol from her stomach which might invalidate the breath test. I get to the 20 minute mark and offer her the breath test. Instead of blowing in the machine, she insists she must use the bathroom again to pee. I don't want to wait another 20 minutes, which is what is required if she leaves my sight, so I try to talk her into blowing into the breathalyzer. Now she is screaming she is going to pee in the floor if I don't let her go immediately. So I get the matron again and let her use the rest room. Finally 20 more minutes pass and I get her to blow into the breath machine. Yep she is as drunk as I thought she was………Got some big number like .30 breath alcohol content which is three times the DUI threshold.

    I relax, now she gets a phone call to try to secure her bond and be released from jail. She calls her 18 year old daughter. Instead of asking for bail money and a ride home, she reads the kid the riot act on how she should not be like her mom and get a DUI. This call goes on for what seemed like ten minutes. Ranting over and over to her kid!

    The call ends and the kid still hasn't been asked to bring bond money for her Mom or provide her a ride home. I give the drunken woman a second call and she gets hold of a man who brings her the bond.

    The only reason I can account that the drunken woman called her daughter was to set her straight. Strange parenting!

CHAPTER 83
WON'T YOU MAKE THAT PHONE CALL?

One afternoon I was on patrol on Il Rt 3 near McClure Illinois in Alexander County. I observed a three axle dump truck running down Il Rt 3 with no visible license plate on the vehicle. I got behind the vehicle and turned on my overhead lights. The driver sped up and turned off Il Rt 3 into McClure.

I was pretty amazed as I had never had someone in a dump truck try to get away. The dump truck pulled beside a mobile home and the driver jumped out and ran inside with me right at his heels. We get to the farthest room in the trailer and he jumps under the bed. His feet were still sticking out from under the bed so I pull the guy out by his legs.

The guy was a pretty easy going guy once I got him from under the bed. He followed my orders and we went outside to my squad car. I questioned the subject and he said he was driving the truck for his son, who owned the company. The driver also admitted he was a suspended driver.

I wrote the fellow two citations. One citation was for the registration and the other was for driving while suspended. (I gave him a break on trying to run away). Illinois requires bond for only the most serious offense and this guy needed $100.00. The driver provided the necessary bond and was released.

Several weeks later, on a dark Friday night, I'm patrolling U.S. Rt. 51 in downtown Cairo, Illinois. Cairo is the county seat of Alexander County. While Cairo is a small town it has serious crime issues. I observe a truck tractor trailer going South on U.S. Rt. 51

with a blown headlight. I activate my overhead lights and the truck stops on the side of the road, right beside a pay phone.

I go up to the truck tractor unit and low and behold it's the same driver who had ducked under his bed in McClure, Illinois. I check and sure enough the driver is still suspended. I again ask for the necessary bond and my driver says he doesn't have the money this time.

I said, "you're in luck, we are beside a pay phone." "Call your son in Mcclure", which is a short distance, "and he will bring you the bond and then drive your truck away."

The driver refused to call his son saying he was asleep at this time of night.

I said call a friend. Call anyone you want but you need a hundred dollars or you will go to jail.

The drive again refused to use the phone.

Now I know what the driver doesn't know. Alexander County jail is one tough place. The jail at this time was in Cairo. It was a small, nasty, place filed with some real tough folks. I know this guy and he is not going to do well as an inmate here.

So I plead with the guy, "won't you please make the phone call."

"No" comes the last reply.

Okay, games over. I place my suspect in handcuffs. I call for a tow and take his truck and trailer away costing him probably $300.00. Finally I transport him to Alexander County jail.

I arrived at the jail finding the jailer swamped as usual on a Friday night. My suspect takes a look into the two cells at the jail and turned white as a ghost. He was figuring out this was a bad place and he has made a real bad decision. Each cell is full and most of the prisoners are tough as nails.

My prisoner adds to his misery by saying, "you're not really going to put me in there with them are you." Naturally all the guys in the cell blocks are not happy that my guy thinks he is too good for their type. Now he wants to make a phone call. The problem is I don't run the jail and the head jailer says he will have to wait for his call.

We got the suspect into the jail cell. All his fellow prisoners were saying things like "what's the matter baby' don't you like us." I suspect this guy learned a huge lesson. Don't drive without a license and make a phone call when given an opportunity.

CHAPTER 84
YAMS

Policing today involves the use of computers. For example, a computer software system called NCIC (which is an acronym for National Crime Information System) is used by most police departments. NCIC is used on almost every traffic stop made in the U.S. As the officer turns on his overhead lights to make a traffic stop, he/she is radioing to his dispatcher the location of the stop, the type of vehicle being stopped, and the license number of the vehicle being stopped. The dispatcher is feeding that information into a computer system with NCIC software. If the vehicle being stopped registration information shows the vehicle is stolen or involved in say a murder, NCIC alerts the dispatcher. The dispatcher then alerts the officer.

Late one night around Christmas 1999, I was on patrol on I57 in Franklin county Illinois. (I 57 is a major interstate running from Texas to Chicago, Illinois. I 57 carries a tremendous amount of goods and therefore has heavy truck traffic.) I observed a truck with a rear trailer light out and made a traffic stop. As I made the stop, the dispatcher made me aware the license plate I had ran on the trailer indicated the unit was stolen.

I went forward and got the operators driver's license. I ran a computer criminal history on the driver. (I was checking with NCIC to see what type of arrest this driver had previously been involved in). The driver had previously been involved in trailer and vehicle theft and had been imprisoned years earlier for these crimes.

I checked the VIN (vehicle identification number) on the trailer. The VIN is a 17 digit combination of numbers and letters that the manufacturer puts on each vehicle. The VIN is the fingerprint so to speak of the vehicle, as each vehicle has only one number and no other vehicle would possess this VIN. The VIN was a match for the stolen trailer.

I had a trailer with an exact match for a stolen vehicle and a former convicted vehicle thief driving it. Certainly probable cause existed for arrest. The driver was insisting he had reformed. He said he had bought this trailer at an insurance pool (here multiple recovered stolen vehicles are kept and then sold to the public by auction). The driver could not produce any paperwork.

I locked the driver up for vehicle theft and had the trailer towed to an impound lot so I could return it to its owner at a later date. A day later I received a call from the driver's wife protesting his innocence. She faxed me some paperwork showing the trailer had been purchased at an insurance pool.

Now any computer system is only as good as those who inter the data. The stolen vehicle report in NCIC was from a small Texas border town near Mexico. The trailer was stolen here and they interred the data into NCIC. Once that data is interred in NCIC, only that same small towns Police Department can remove it.

As I checked on the trailer, I found after it was stolen, it had been recovered, in Boston Massachusetts. The insurance company had paid off the trucking company for the stolen trailer so when it was recovered it belonged to the insurance company. The insurance company sold the trailer to this driver I had stopped. Boston had notified the small Texas town of the trailers recovery but that town had not removed the stolen information from NCIC.

I had jailed an innocent man based on bad computer information. So I went to the states attorney and got permission to release the driver.

All my work had taken time and it was now New Year's Day. I got the driver from jail and took him to his truck tractor unit and he was understandably upset. He explained he had invested $60,000 dollars in yams and then he asked me what he was to do with them. I asked what he meant and he explained yams were a hot item only twice a year; Christmas and New Year's Day. Now he had a trailer load of yams and no one to sell them to

I suggested he file a lawsuit against the Texas town as they had put him this situation. I have no idea how this ended, I suppose his yams were marketed at a very low price.

CHAPTER 85
YOU THREW MY SISTER LIKE A BAG OF TATERS

Alcohol does strange things to people's minds. A little alcohol loosens people up. With a few drinks, the timid get a little confidence. With heavy drinking, comes a major change in people's character. The Bible declares, "Wine is a mocker and strong drink a brawler." This is as true today as it was the day it was written. Wine drinkers act stupid and are no threat to the police. A drinker of strong drink (i.e. whiskey, vodka, etc.) will be very dangerous to those around him. That danger extends to the police as well.

This story begins as I ended my shift around 10 P.M. I was traveling I57 and had a few minutes to spare before pulling into my driveway to go off shift. I decided to run a few extra miles looking for someone needing a motorist assist. By this time in my career, I had learned that stopping cars just before the shift ended often resulted in hours of overtime. The car you might pick for a simple speeding ticket might have a suspended driver or wanted suspect inside. Cars that were broken down on the side of the road were less likely to require overtime. I would call for a tow truck or jump the car and be gone.

Tonight wasn't my night. I found a pickup truck pulled to the roadways edge. I suspected this was simply a broken down car needing assistance. As I approached the truck, I could see the vehicle had been recently off the highway. The trucks rear bumper was full of vegetation and its tires were full of mud. A mud track could be seen on the highway leading to the truck.

I get to the door and speak to the driver. The driver was an older white male. I would guess his age as 62. The driver is very intoxicated. The front seat passenger is a female of about the same age. The woman has urinated in her pants and the truck smells of alcohol and urine. The driver identifies the drunken woman as his sister. The driver says his truck won't run. I go to the front of the truck and it is clear why the truck won't run. The front end has been crashed into what may have been multiple items. The radiator is knocked out and the front bumper area is bent in toward the driver. I also notice the truck contains a small Chihuahua dog.

Well, its overtime tonight I tell myself.

I check the driver for sobriety and he is as drunk as I initially thought. The driver is so drunk I have to assist him on his sobriety test to keep him from falling over. I place the guy under arrest for DUI and handcuff him. I put him in my car and radio post to send me a tow truck.

The tow truck arrives and begins to attach the tow lines to the old man's truck. About that time, the tow driver appears at my squad car door. The tow truck driver says the old woman is refusing to get out of the pickup. The tow driver says he cannot and will not tow the pickup with her still inside. The tow driver is afraid the woman will jump or fall out of the towed vehicle.

A note to the reader here. The tow truck drivers would not only tow the cars but provide a seat in their tow truck for passengers. The passenger would be dropped off at a restaurant or motel in route to the tow yard, where the towed vehicle would be stored.

I tell the tow driver I will speak to the old woman. I go forward and explain that she must go to the tow truck passenger seat and ride there during the tow operation. The old woman is very belligerent and tells me she will not leave the truck. I play on her sympathy and speak to her about taking care of the Chihuahua. She repeats she will not leave the pickup. Finally I explain I will have to arrest her if she fails to leave the pickup and get in the tow truck. I explain she is obstructing a police officer.

The old woman tells me to get f***** and grabs the dashboard. I grab her by the belt loop on the back of her jeans but the belt loop breaks. I grab her by the back of the pants themselves and her shirt. This woman has a death grip on the dash and so far she is not budging. Finally I break her grip on the dash and out the door she comes into the weeds beside the road. I go to handcuff her and she is yelling she is paralyzed.

I run back to my squad car and call for an ambulance and a dog catcher. I ask tor the night Sergeant to come to the scene of this stop.

The little old man sitting beside me is obviously irate. He looks at me and says, "I saw what you just did. You threw my sister like a bag of taters into those weeds."

I started to explain to the man that his sister had refused multiple requests to get out of the truck. I was going to tell him how she locked her legs and arms in such away as I had to pry her out. Then I came to my senses. You cannot explain things to a drunk. So I waited with the old woman for her ambulance.

The ambulance came and took the old woman away. She was faking her injuries. Drunk as she was, she was sure she did not want to go to jail. The hospital looked like a better alternative to her.

The old man went to jail. The Sergeant showed up and watched my video of the old woman being pulled from the pickup. The Sergeant said I was within my scope of duty to remove her forcefully to arrest her.

I stopped by the tow service and met with the tow operator who towed the pickup. The driver filled out a voluntary statement as to what transpired the previous night with the old lady and old man. The driver did have this to say. He said I've been towing cars for years and never had one like that one.

Truer words have never been spoken!

CHAPTER 86
WARNING – STORIES BEYOND THIS CONTAIN INSTANCES OF DEATH

The stories beyond this point contain instances of death and dismemberment. I debated whether or not to write stories that contain instances of death. The American public, by and large, have never seen a person die. Death, when it occurs, is hidden from the American public. Nurses, doctors, EMT's, firemen, and police see death regularly but the general public does not. Why is it, we have given certain occupations the need to see death but not the public at large? Below is my opinion of why we hide death.

Most people do not want to see the dead. I suppose we have our own fears of dying and don't want to be reminded of our mortality. Yes we are all going to die but seeing a person die makes us uncomfortable.

Dead people are often gross. Dead people usually either have a bad malady or are dismembered in an accident and they are hard to look at. Those who die of cancer or disease change color, loose a great amount of weight, or have their bodies rot. Most people don't do well with these changes. We want people to look healthy. If the death is a result of dismemberment, it is worse. Here we have a person who appears to be in good health that has now been crushed, cut, or otherwise put in pieces. Most Americans no longer hunt or see animals dissected so seeing a human being in pieces upsets them.

Americans are a tidy people. We can take death if we must go to a funeral home. The dead person in a funeral home has been washed, had makeup applied, and is wearing fine clothes. Often the dead person in the casket looks better than they did in real life.

If you choose to go beyond this page the stories are pretty graphic. I was a cop so I saw death. I probably saw more than most cops as I was a Commercial Motor Vehicle Officer (CVEO) for 12 years.

If there was a death or serious injury caused by a Commercial Motor Vehicle (i.e. large truck), I had to respond. My hours of response were from two o'clock in the afternoon till five o'clock in the morning. My area of response included some of the most heavily traveled interstate highways in the nation. Due to my hours of coverage and location I have seen many, many, deaths due to car/truck crashes. In these crashes the occupants of the smaller cars are often torn to pieces.

The effect on me of being around so much death has been to develop a hard exterior. Some call the hard exterior "police humor". Police humor helps those who deal with death on a regular basis to keep their sanity. I am sure you will see some police humor as I write. Please excuse me as I do not wish to offend you but feel some of the police humor has its place to educate you as to the way "police humor" sounds.

CHAPTER 87
EXPLODING BATTERIES AND A BURNING MAN

This story is a tough one to write. It involves friendship and death. It involves a horrendous truck crash. It is true and needs to be told if he reader is to understand what Troopers face.

I was at a church ice cream social in the middle of July when I received a call to a multiple truck crash on I57 just north of the West Frankfort, Illinois exit. I rushed home, which was only a few blocks away, got into my uniform, and drove to the crash scene.

I've lost ten minutes getting to the crash. As I arrive, I see two truck tractor trailer rigs loaded with asphalt that are front to back to each other. The rear asphalt truck has hit the front asphalt truck in the rear. The front asphalt truck is on fire. The driver of the front asphalt truck is apparently passed out with his head out his driver's window with his truck burning. Further ahead of the two trucks is a third truck which is hauling car batteries. The third truck has lost batteries all over the roadway. The batteries are loaded with battery acid. The road is so hot from it being July and the asphalt fire that the batteries are exploding like bombs. The batteries sound like bombs as they explode and are throwing acid ten or fifteen feet high as they go off.

I jump from my car and the driver of the rear asphalt hauling unit is screaming his friend in the front asphalt truck is burning up. I avoid exploding batteries and get to the front truck. The truck's load of asphalt is on fire and trucks diesel fuel system is also burning. I can't get any closer than five feet to the truck due to the heat. If I try to go any closer, I feel my skin being burned. I yell to a fireman who has just arrived to put on a fire coat and try a rescue. The fireman tries but he cannot take the heat even with his protective coat. We watch the man melt in front of our eyes.

I settle the rear truck driver into my squad car, out of the hot July sun. I run to the battery truck. The battery truck was hit in the rear by the front asphalt truck. Damage to the battery truck is confined to the rear of the unit. I expect the operator of the battery truck to be uninjured. The battery truck driver is dead. The man died of an apparent heart attack; perhaps brought on by the accident. I call the fireman over for an attempted rescue with an AED. The battery truck driver cannot be resuscitated.

I go back to my squad car. The driver of the back asphalt truck is wailing and crying. It turns out; he and his best friend (the driver of the front asphalt truck) were talking on the citizens band radio as they hauled asphalt up the interstate highway. The rear driver said he did not see traffic braking and hit his friend's truck in the rear. My driver said his friend then crashed his truck into the battery truck. My driver said he had killed his friend.

How does someone console this at fault driver? I knew he did not deliberately hurt anyone; much less his best friend. Yet he was correct in that he had caused his friends death.

I had to do a job. By policy I had to write a citation to the at fault driver in a death accident. It was the toughest ticket I ever wrote. My heart went out to the driver.

The next day I'm at the tow yard still working on the previous days trucks. I was busy measuring the brakes to be sure they were in compliance with federal truck brake laws. The driver who caused yesterday's truck crash shows up with a little eight year old boy. The boy is distraught and crying. The driver explained he needed some items he had left in his truck yesterday.

I allowed the driver to get his personal belongings from the truck. I asked him if he intended to drive a truck in the future. I asked this knowing most companies would not hire him as a result of this crash.

The driver said, "He would not drive anymore." He said his first job was to take care of the little boy he had brought with him. The driver said the boy was the son to his friend who died in yesterday's crash.

I felt like crying for this driver. He was doing what he could now to take care of his friend's son. Life is sometimes very tough!

CHAPTER 88
JIMMY JOE KILLS HIMSELF AND 5 OTHERS

Seldom does a State Trooper meet a suspect more than once. Sometimes when a Trooper runs traffic in the small towns of Southern Illinois it will happen but seldom or never on the interstate. This is a story of meeting a man not once but twice on the interstate. The second meeting was beyond belief.

My story starts in 2005. I was running radar in Williamson County. This was before there was a steel cable median barrier between Northbound and Southbound lanes of traffic. I would drive my squad car in the passing lane of southbound traffic and perform moving radar on the northbound traffic. If I observed a vehicle traveling at a high rate of speed, I would cause my squad car to go through the median and turn around and chase the violator's vehicle down. On this day I was at the bottom of the large hill just South of Marion, Illinois. I used my radar to check the speed of a flatbed truck tractor combination and it was 78 miles per hour in a 55 miles per hour zone.

I shot through the median and got behind the truck and got it to stop just on top of the hill which is on the South boundary of Marion. The driver came out like a madman. I got his Tennessee license and put up with his screaming mouth throughout the stop. I did not let him stop me from doing my job. This driver who I will call Jimmy Joe got a speeding citation and a truck inspection. His behavior was such that I felt he might attack me but he did not.

I let Jimmy Joe go on his way and I noticed a different truck tractor with a load that was not properly secured go past me. I got the second truck stopped. This truck was driven by an old man from Tennessee. When I brought the old man to my squad car for a truck inspection he noticed my portable laptop computer which set on a stand inside my squad car. The old gentleman asked what the page was that was displaying on my computer screen.

I explained that this page came from all the different truck inspections that I had performed in the last month. The page gave the date and time of the stop, the trucking company involved, the name of the driver of the truck, and what state the driver's license came from.

The old man looked at my screen. He noticed my last driver stopped before him was named Joe and he was also from Tennessee. He asked if that driver was Jimmy Joe who was near 50 years old from a certain part of Tennessee. When I replied yes do you know him, the old gentleman came unglued. He said this Jimmy Joe was always in trouble and had been in and out of jail most of his life. He gave me a different birth last name that Jimmy had used most of his life. He said Jimmy only changed his name after coming out of prison his last time so as to improve his credit.

I took down the last name the old man gave me and checked it to see if Jimmy Joe had beaten the system by getting a driver's license under the last name "Joe" while really being suspended under his birth name. The check showed Jimmy was not suspended under his birth name and so when he legally changed his last name he could get a valid license with his new name. There was nothing more I could do with Jimmy; he was a valid Tennessee driver.

Several months after my stop of Jimmy Joe, I received a phone call from a Trooper near Effingham, Illinois. He too had stopped Jimmy Joe and the fur flew on this stop also. This Trooper said he had thought he was going to be attacked by Jimmy Joe and had written a report to label him in our computer system as a safety risk. The Trooper had checked and had seen where I had written jimmy

Joe a speeding citation and that Jimmy had gotten court supervision on it.

Court supervision is like getting probation. The speeding citation I wrote Jimmy would not go on his driving record in Tennessee unless Williamson County forwarded it to them. Williamson county would check Jimmy's driving record 90 days after he plead court supervision and if he had no further convictions then no record of this citation would go to Tennessee and no points would go on Jimmy's driving record. If jimmy got another conviction during the 90 days then Williamson County would forward the speeding citation information to Tennessee.

The Trooper calling wanted me to call the Williamson County States Attorney and have them revoke Jimmy's court supervision because he acted a jerk when this Trooper stopped him.

I gave the calling Trooper the phone number to the Williamson County States Attorney. I realized the Trooper's request was not going to happen. Court Supervision is revoked only by a second conviction and not by difficult behavior on the part of a driver.

On January 25, 2006, in the afternoon, I got a call to a multiple vehicle crash on I57 at the bottom of the hill just south of Marion, Illinois. When I arrived it looked like a war zone. A flatbed truck tractor driven by Jimmy Joe was traveling southbound on the interstate. The flatbed was carrying loads of coiled steel. The driver lost control and had shot across the interstate median. Jimmy's truck took the rear trailer wheels off a second truck. That truck went down into a portion of the big muddy river that flows under the interstate. The driver swam to safety. Jimmy's truck then clipped a UPS truck in its front end. The hit took off the UPS trucks passenger side front bumper area. Then Jimmy's truck plowed head on into a pickup truck containing 5 people. The pickup had two adults and three children inside. In addition to the hit of Jimmy's truck, the pickup caught the weight of a large coil of steel that shifted when the crash occurred.

When I arrived the fire fighters were on scene and were freeing Jimmy form the crash. He appeared to be trying to fight his rescuers. Inside the pickup only one child was alive and was being rescued. The child and Jimmy died in Marion's hospital emergency room according to reports.

I did the investigation of all three large trucks. Jimmy Joe's driving record was the most interesting of my findings. He had managed to be arrested five times for excessive speed but had not yet lost his driving privileges. Jimmy had probably plead not guilty to several citations and pushed the dates back on his trials so he could drive longer before a suspension set in.

This wreck was traumatic as three young girls died. The results of this wreck were numerous. Illinois Department of Transportation came in and put a median barrier using steel cable between Marion Illinois and the area south of the big hill. Court supervision was no longer offered to truck drivers. Now points would be assessed for all speeding violations. Finally the U. S. Department of Transportation began to follow truck drivers driving records far more closely than before this crash.

I wish I could say something good about what I learned from this crash. I cannot. What I learned was what I already knew, "people who drive with no regards to others often kill them."

CHAPTER 89
OLD PEOPLES BONES

I am not a medical doctor. I was a Trooper and what I observed about the bones of older people has no scientific basis. With that disclaimer let me give you a very graphic story about old bones.

I had been at my post in DuQuoin taking a class in self-defense. I was riding with another Trooper and we were traveling on Il Rt 14 and had just passed through Christopher, Illinois heading toward Buckner, Illinois. Traffic slowed and looking beyond the line of traffic in our lane, I could see we had rolled upon a new car crash.

I got out of the squad car and went forward to the crash. A roll back tow truck had hit head on with an older model Chevrolet. While the crash was head on, it was at a slight angle. It turned out the tow truck had been passing another vehicle and had hit the Chevrolet head on but at an angle. The crash left the Chevrolet in the middle of the highway but the tow truck was down a ravine.

As I walked toward the Chevrolet, I met the Franklin county States Attorney. The States attorney just happened to be driving on the highway when the crash occurred but was in no way personally involved. He looks at me and he appears very shaken. He blurts out this is a bad one and quickly exits my area. I continue to walk forward two girls are beside the Chevrolet and are throwing up. I asked if they were involved in the crash. The girls say no and point to the Chevrolet.

I look inside the Chevrolet and I see a man with a glass bowl on his head. In reality, there was no glass bowl. I have discovered when I see something surreal my mind seeks to make sense of a terrible scene. What I was seeing was a man whose scull has been busted off at the top. I was looking down inside where his brain should be at. The top of the scull and the brain are gone. What is left is a hollo cup of a head with nothing inside.

I look into the back of the car near the windshield area; the area is like a back dash on the car. There I see the top of the man's scull and his brain. The crash had been so hard it was as if someone had taken an electric saw and had cut the top of his head off.

I had seen such scenes before. I theorized that this older man (in his 80's) had "very brittle bones." I could see that he had hit his head violently on the cars steering wheel. (The car was older model and the steering wheel was not as cushioned as the newer models.) The result was the older man very brittle bones busted off as if they had been sawed with an electric saw.

Seeing the man was deceased, I went to check on the driver of the tow truck. Amazingly the tow truck operator was uninjured.

By now the ambulance crew had arrived. The ambulance crew consisted of one male and two females. The odd number of ambulance personnel was due to one of the females being an intern and not a full Emergency Medical Technician.

I was busy directing traffic when the male ambulance driver comes to me and asks my assistance in removing the old man's body from the Chevrolet. I put some people at the scene in charge of traffic control and go with the ambulance driver to the Chevrolet. There is no evidence that any effort has been made to extract the dead man.

I look at the young ambulance driver and ask why with three people he cannot remove the dead body from the Chevrolet?

The young man replies his two assistants are sick and are throwing up. He says unless someone helps him he will be unable to get the guy out. He says you know how it is with a dead person's weight.

I look at my pristine uniform and decide I don't want to wear the dead guy's blood. Picking this guy up could cost me a uniform for months as I await a replacement uniform that has to be sent from Springfield, Illinois. So I ask the young man if he has a plastic bag and some twine.

The Young man finds a plastic shopping bag somewhere and some twine and returns. I bag the dead guy's head and tie off the bag around the neck to prevent blood from getting on me as we remove the body. It was a heavy lift but we got the dead man from his car and on a gurney.

I expected the twine around the dead man's neck would cause me grief. The twine around the dead man's neck would make it appear someone had been choking this man with the twine at the time of the crash. I suppose the coroner figured this out as I never heard from him and the incident was closed. I suppose the saying "necessity is the mother of all invention" applies here as I kept my uniform clean and got the dead man moved to the gurney.

CHAPTER 90
SEEING MY FIRST DEAD PERSON ON THE JOB

I had been a police officer for eight years. I had been a Secretary of State Policeman (SOS Police) and later an Illinois Commerce Commission Police (ILCC Police) officer. The SOS Police enforce title and registration laws. The SOS Police do some traffic stops but do not handle accidents. Similarly the ILCC handles trucking laws and makes traffic stops but does not do accidents. So with eight years of policing under my belt I had yet to be up close and personal with a dead man.

When I was accepted into the Illinois State Police in 1995, I had to return to the academy and be retrained. One of the areas of retraining was in traffic crashes. I was also shown what seemed like hundreds of videos of crashes where people were dismembered. The Illinois State Police (ISP) was trying to desensitize me to what a dismembered body looked like.

Once I finished the academy, I spent ten weeks riding with different older State Policemen to learn the ropes of being a Trooper. I was working with an older Trooper near Marion, Illinois. The older Trooper received a call and without letting me know the calls content he took me about forty miles to a town called Chester, Illinois. We entered a hospital where a Sergeant was waiting. The Sergeant had brought with him an intern. The intern was a SIU (Southern Illinois University) student wanting to try to get employment with us upon graduating.

The Sergeant explained a young man had just been killed in a traffic crash. The guy had been intoxicated and stayed out all night.

Still intoxicated when morning had come, he drove his car off the road and hit a tree. The Sergeant said the young man was in the next room. The Sergeant wanted me, the new Trooper, and the intern to view the body of the deceased.

All three of us, the Sergeant, the intern and I, entered the hospital room with the deceased young man. Surprisingly to me the dead man was in good shape. I looked the dead guy over. His eyes were blackened; like you would see when someone gets a shiner. I explained to the intern that the orbits behind the eye had been shattered when this guy's car hit the tree. I also pointed to the clear fluid running from the diseased ears. I explained this was fluid that came from the brain was called amniotic fluid. At this the intern shot from the room. The intern was sick to his stomach. I looked around and I was the only person in the room. The Sergeant had left without my knowing it.

I looked over the dead man for more signs of what killed him. I could not find any other injuries and decided he must have died from the brain injury I had seen clues to. I exited the room and met with the Sergeant and the older trooper who had brought me to the hospital. I asked the Sergeant why I had been brought some forty miles to view a dead man.

The Sergeant replied, "we wanted to see if you could handle seeing death."

I said, "I guess I did okay then."

The Sergeant admitted I had handled being around a dead guy well.

I then asked Old Sarge, "why didn't you stay in the room with me." I was thinking he wanted me to be alone with the dead guy to see how I did.

Surprisingly Sarge said, "I really don't like to be alone with dead people."

I thought this is a fine situation. I'm expected to do okay around dead people and the guy making me do it doesn't do well with dead people. Go figure!

CHAPTER 91
THE END

My father was a very wise man. Whenever he met someone contemplating retirement he would always say, "Make sure you get enough water from the well the first time because you can't go back again." This meant do not retire till you are sure the money your retirement brings in will be sufficient because you won't be able to return to work to fix the deficiency. As I got near the end of my State Police employment, I always considered my father's words.

Most State Policemen enjoy the work when they first take on the position. The officer is young and the challenge is exciting. Running down criminals on foot, chasing them in high speed pursuits, and pulling weapons in self-defense all give an adrenaline dump that is hard to describe. As the officer ages the job takes a toll. Seeing people torn to pieces in car crashes, injuring one another, stealing, and hating their fellow man all begin to take a toll. Finally, as the officer closes in on the end of his/her career, the realization that a younger man might literally rip your head off or steal your gun, or in some other way kill you sets in. You realize this as it happens to others around you.

Like most officers with around the twenty year of service mark I began to want to retire. I was told that 20 years would allow me to retire with insurance so I drove to Springfield, Illinois to meet with my retirement counselor. The gentleman agreed I had sufficient time to retire but asked a question that haunted me. He said are you willing to give up 18% of your pay for the rest of your life. My father's warning rang through my ears. The money was sufficient at the time but would it be sufficient later. I told the man "no I would not be willing to give up so much money." I asked how long before I returned. The gentleman said five years.

Five years later I returned to Springfield and met with the same retirement counselor. I said I had returned on his recommendation. I was reasonably sure I was finished. I was 55 years old and the idea of having to fight off a 20 year old no longer seemed wise. The gentleman did the math on my retirement and he came back to me. The man said are you willing to give up 8% of your possible retirement earnings for the rest of your life. Again I said "no."

I asked when I should return. The gentleman showed me a chart showing I would be very near the end of my career on April 2012. So we agreed to meet then.

Several of my colleagues had already quit and encouraged me to do the same. One reminded me of the danger of our work and told me to retire or as he said it "call it a day". He said he had just taken the loss as the money was no longer worth it to him.

I stuck it out until April of 2012. I now had 26 years of service time. I knew from speaking to the counselor that I was 8 months short of full retirement. I was 56 years old and even the rifle shoots which involved running and falling down to shoot and picking yourself up and running some more were no longer fun. So I drove back to see the counselor. The man said you are 1.3% short of full retirement what do you say. I said "I'm done."

I had gotten so close to the very end that 1.3% did not matter. I had outlasted most but not all of those officers who hired on when I did. I had kept my father's wisdom. I had stayed at the well long enough to cover my life in retirement.

Made in the USA
Coppell, TX
20 March 2021